Games for All Ages

AND HOW TO USE THEM

Games for All Ages

AND HOW TO USE THEM

by MARJORIE WACKERBARTH
and
LILLIAN S. GRAHAM

BAKER BOOK HOUSE
Grand Rapids, Michigan

Reprinted 1973 by Baker Books
a division of Baker Book House Company
P.O. Box 6287, Grand Rapids, MI 49516-6287

Library of Congress Catalog Card Number: 5959-13578

ISBN: 0-8010-9536-0

Sixteenth printing, November 1995

Printed in the United States of America

TO
JAMES II, BOB, GRAHAM,
FRANK, CARL and JAMES I

Acknowledgments

We gratefully acknowledge permission from the following magazines to reprint the games used in the stories which we have written for them.

AMERICAN HOME

A Party for Boisterous Boys
A Stag for Thirteeners
A Teen-Age Party
The Goblins Will Get You

CALLING ALL GIRLS

Flowers in February

CHRISTIAN MOTHER

Start with Starch
Party for Tricycle Set

COUNTRY GENTLEMAN

Make it a Family Affair
Reprinted by special permission from Country Gentleman magazine, copyright, 1949, by The CURTIS PUBLISHING COMPANY

FARM JOURNAL

The First Boy-Girl Party
Kiddie Cat Prowl
Rainbow's Pot of Gold
Tail-catching stunt

HOSPITALITY HOME

Fun for Little Lonesome

McCALL'S

"No Sissy Games"

REDBOOK

Fun for Small Fry

STAR WEEKLY OF TORONTO

Fun for the Sick Child
Invite the Parents Too
A Magician's Party
Halloween Bean-O
Back to School Party
Party in Outer Space

TRUE CONFESSIONS

Birthdays Must Be Celebrated

WEE WISDOM

Dorothy's Halloween Party
A Thanksgiving Party

WORKBENCH

Dogs Brighten a Basement Room's Walls.

Acknowledgment is also given to Mrs. Ruth David, Teen-age program director of the Minneapolis, Minnesota, YWCA for game information. We also want to express appreciation to Mabel Otis Robison and Sylvia Sanders for help in locating game material, and to our many friends who have given us their favorite games.

Contents

Introduction

Games can be fun for everyone. They are the spice that enlivens the tediousness of sitting still in a classroom. They are the magic that changes physical training into enjoyable competition. They are the ingredient that turns a dull party into loads of fun.

Games are universal in their appeal. Cavemen's children probably invented the first games by seeing who could throw rocks the farthest—the ancestor of our shot-put. Sidewalk hopscotch enjoyed by our city children probably was first scratched out in desert sand. Almost the same games can be found in every country and every land.

Toys have changed with the mechanized age, but games remain primarily the same. Adaptations of old favorites to fit the theme of a party or a special occasion give an original flavor to some games. Others we repeat from telling, still others are found in the game literature of the day, the authorship of which has been lost by the wayside. If the original source is known, credit is given to the author.

SUGGESTIONS FOR GAME PROGRAMS

If you are planning a party at home, an entertainment for a church group or a club, or recreational work for a school class, choice of games and arrangement of material are important. But the most vital factor in your program planning is the leader. The person who helps others have a good time must approach the group with the expectancy of fun—fun for himself and fun for the group. Such enthusiasm radiates joyousness, and is contagious. The players reflect the spirit of the leader.

If the program leader follows a few general rules, his path is easier and he will be successful.

1—As a leader, understand thoroughly the game you are explaining. Make your directions brief and clear. If necessary, demonstrate the action.

2—Stand where all can see you. Speak so that you can be heard, but don't shout. Expect the players to listen. If your group is large, use a low-pitched whistle sparingly. A high, shrill whistle is frequently drowned out by the high-pitched voices of children.

3—For the first game, choose one that is familiar to most of the group—one that is easy to explain in a few words. Go into the game without hesitation, and get the group actively interested from the start. More difficult games can be explained after the players are more confident and relaxed. This is especially true of adults or even older young people, who frequently are self-conscious about games.

4—Stop a game while everyone is enthusiastic about it. Never continue a game until even a few players are bored with it. Enthusiasm will carry over to the next game.

5—Play the game yourself, or at least watch with lively interest. Remember the leader's enthusiasm is most contagious.

The second requirement for successful entertainment is a program plan. The program will be easier for the leader, and more fun for the group if certain basic rules are followed.

1. Plan your game program in detail. Make a list of games in order of play so that you may progress from one game to another without delay.

2. Plan an abundance of games. For children the average game lasts about seven minutes. Some will run longer, of course, but it is better to have too many games on tap than to run short.

3. Plan your games to avoid exhaustion and confusion. Alternate active games with quiet ones. Let your formations follow through—a circle game after a circle game—a line game after a line game.

4. Play an exceptionally good game just before refreshments. In case of a home party, the enthusiasm for the game will give the leader a chance to make last minute preparations before serving refreshments. And in a large group the enthusiasm for the game will carry over the intermission.

5. Finish the program with a game that you are sure will make a hit. Stop the game at its height, sing "Good night, ladies," and end the program decisively.

These basic rules for a good leader and game programming are helpful in planning a large community party, a smaller group party of approximately thirty people, or for a small home party of a dozen or so young guests.

I.

Mixers

The first fifteen minutes of a party is a crucial period. If early arrivals stand around idle, even if for only a short time, they are apt to feel self-conscious and shy. To avoid this, launch a game as soon as the very first guests arrive— a game in which late comers can join without noticeable interruption. Such games are called Mixers. Here are some delightful ones.

FRIENDLY FACES

As the guests arrive, each person is given a tag with his name on it to wear on his lapel. Request each guest to memorize as quickly as possible the names of his fellow guests. Then ask each guest to remove his own name tag, and give him a blank card and pencil.

Direct the players to write on the cards the names of as many guests as they can remember in five minutes. The longest list wins and is read aloud. Also, the shortest list is read.

PAPER HEADS

As the guests arrive, give each person a paper sack, a number, a card on which to write and a pencil. The guest pins the number on himself, tears holes for eyes in the paper sack and slips it over his head. Then with a card and pencil he begins to identify as many of the party as possible by listing the number and name of each paper head.

Another way to handle this game is to prepare the sacks as masks ahead of time. No. 20 is the proper size of sack to use. Cut notches for eyes, nose and mouth, and crayon a large number just above the eyes. A few pencil marks in the right places make these masks appear smiling, grotesque, or funny. The sack will fit the head better if the bottom edge of the back is torn up a bit to fit onto the neck. The mask effect of the paper heads adds considerably to the fun of the game.

MEMORY LANE

The boys (or half the group) form an outside circle, the girls (or the rest of the group) make an inside circle. Each boy writes on the pad of the girl in front of him all the girls' names he can think of beginning with "A." When the whistle blows within thirty seconds, he moves to the girl on his right and lists for her all the names he can think of beginning with "B." The girls may not help their partners. The girl with the longest list wins.

After the boys have moved five times they may be told to keep the pad on which they are writing. The girls are then asked to move to the right. They are

then to list on the boys' pad all the boys' names beginning with "F." The next move they use "G," etc., until
they have moved five places. Then the longest list is
read once again.

NAME CHAIN

Name chain is a good way for a group of less than
twenty-five to learn each others' names. The first person turns to the second and gives his own name. The
second repeats this and adds his own name. The third
repeats the first and second name and adds his own.
And so on around the circle.

PAPER LETTERS

From ads in newspapers select the names of foods.
For instance, take the word "Butter," and cut it into
separate letters. As the guest arrives, give him an envelope containing all the letters of one word. He must
unscramble the word and know which food he has. He
then writes his word on a slip of paper and wears it for
the evening. The scholarly guest invariably winds up
wearing "Nuts," and the fat boy "Skim milk."

LAUGHING HANDKERCHIEF

All the guests sit in a circle. "It" holds a handkerchief in the air while everyone laughs. The harder
you laugh the more fun it is. Without warning, "It"
drops the hanky. When the hanky hits the floor everyone is supposed to stop laughing and immediately put

on a "straight face." The last one to stop laughing becomes "It." This is lots of fun.

IRISH BLARNEY

Let each arriving guest draw a number from a hat —green for boys and white for girls with corresponding numbers. When everyone has arrived, the leaders call out a boy's number, asking him to tell his unknown partner what he considers the loveliest thing about her. When he has finished his blarney the much complimented girl with the number corresponding to his will step to his side.

The next boy whose number is called may describe the "Willowy slenderness" of his partner. When his corresponding number steps out, she may turn out to be the chunky young girl who is his next door neighbor. This continues until all the guests have been paired off, the leader selecting a different subject each time.

AMNESIA

For this old favorite be prepared with slips of paper on which the name of comic-strip characters are written. Pin one on the back of each guest without his seeing the name. According to the game, each guest has lost his memory and is to learn his identity himself. He is forbidden to remove the paper from his back or look into a mirror. He can ask questions of the other guests, but only questions that can be answered by "yes" or "no." With everyone asking questions of everyone else, the ice is soon broken.

SCRAMBLED PROVERBS

Before the party begins, type or write a number of proverbs, each one on a separate card. Then cut the cards into several pieces, scramble them, and put six or seven pieces into each envelope Hand an envelope to each guest as he enters. The guests are told to get as many complete proverbs as possible by trading and collecting.

This is an ideal Halloween game if you use superstitions instead of proverbs. Here are some familiar superstitions to use.

1—A broken mirror will bring you seven years of bad luck.

2—If you sing before breakfast, you will cry before night.

3—If a black cat crosses your path, you will have bad luck.

4—To walk under a ladder is extremely bad luck.

5—You'll never finish anything started on Friday.

6—If you put on a garment wrong side out, it's bad luck to change.

7—It's bad luck to sneeze before breakfast.

8—It's bad luck to rock an empty chair.

9—It's bad luck to open an umbrella in the house.

10—It's bad luck to pass anyone on the stairs.

CHAIR VERSES

Do you have a knack for rhyme making? If so, make a rhyme with each one containing a bit of description that fits each guest. Fasten one to a chair and have everyone find his own chair. The hunt for seats, comparing the verses with the guessing involved, makes this game a good mixer. Here are some samples:

For the boy named "Graham," who is good in English, the verse might read:

"This name is a cracker of golden brown.
This guy is a writer known all around town."

For the chatterbox girl:

"She's short and dark with a gift for chatter,
She's not getting younger, but she's sure getting fatter."

For the boy who is on the track team:

"He's witty, clever, and often will sprint
Surely you can guess who with that broad hint."

PICTURE HUNT

From each guest, some time before the party, obtain his baby picture or a picture taken when he was very young. Post these around the room with a number below each picture. Give the guests cards and have them list the pictures by number and name. When all guests are present, ask each one to identify his own baby picture. The player with the most nearly correct list wins.

EYE COLOR

This game will appeal most to older teen-agers or young adults. Armed with card and pencil each person lists the names of the guests and the color of their eyes. The individual with the most complete list wins.

NAME ACROSTICS

Give pencils and cards to each guest as he enters and tell him to print his first name in capitals vertically at the extreme left of his card. The guests mix in the crowd trying to find persons whose first names begin with the letters on his card. For example, Helen's card might be completed with these names:

> H arold
>
> E dna
>
> L ynne
>
> E arl
>
> N ora

No guest's name may be used more than once, unless two or more guests bear the same name. The completed acrostic based on the longest name wins the prize.

COOPERATIVE SPELLING

For a large group this game is an especially good mixer. Each guest fastens onto his arm a large card bearing a letter of the alphabet. He is also given a small card and a pencil. The letters are to get together to spell words. For instance, the one wearing "A" tries to find two others wearing "C" and "T" to form the word "CAT." These three then write "Cat" on each of their cards. Then they separate and seek others with whom they can form a word. The person having the longest list may win a prize, or the prize can be awarded to the members of the group who formed the longest word.

OLD HOG SNEEZE

Divide players into groups of three. First player says "A-hishee," second "A-hashee," and third "A-hoshee" in 1-2-3 order. Repeat several times, then all together. This is an hilarious ice-breaker.

NAME DROP

The entire group forms a circle. Everyone writes his name on a sheet of paper. When the music starts the entire circle marches around clockwise. When the music stops each person drops the slip bearing his name on the floor in front of him. When the music starts the entire circle marches counter-clockwise. When the music stops each one picks up from the floor the name in front of him. Then each player tries to locate the person whose name he has just picked up.

BALLOON BUMP

Each person is given a balloon to tie around his waist so that the balloon is in back of him. The object of the game is for the players to try to break each other's balloon by bumping into one another.

IMPRESSIONS

Each player is asked to spot someone in the crowd whom he doesn't know. The leader tells the players to write down on a card five items such as: **Movie Actor, Car, Food, Song, Dances.** Each player approach-

es the person he has spotted and visits with him for
five minutes without discussing any of the five subjects listed.

At the end of a five-minute discussion, each player
writes on his own card what he **thinks** his partner
thinks of the five items in question. These are then
read aloud. An excellent mixer for teen-agers or adults.

HUMAN BINGO

Each player is given an eight-by-ten inch plain
white card marked off into squares. Each person puts
his own name in the center square. Then the players
move around, asking various individuals to write his
name in some square in their card. When the cards
are full, the caller calls out the name of a person. If
the crowd is large, and the players are strange to one
another, ask each individual called to raise his hand
to identify himself. As the names are called, each player puts an "X" over that name on his card. The first
one to have a complete line of "X's" in any direction
calls out "Bingo" and wins the prize. Two or three
prizes will prolong the game.

ANIMAL DESCRIPTIONS

As your guests arrive, give each one a blank card
and request that they write their initials on it, such as
J. A. W., or B. M. E. After all the guests have initialed
their cards, suggest that they exchange cards with the
nearest person. Then ask each guest to write down
the name of an animal beginning with the last of the

three initials on his card, and two descriptive words about the animal, using the first two initials. For instance, the holder of the card bearing J. A. W. might write "Jumping Athletic Warthog," and the holder of the card bearing B. M. E. might write "Big Mulish Elephant." These cards are then returned to the one whose initials they bear to be read aloud. The game creates great fun.

LAUGH AWAY THE STIFFNESS

If your crowd seems stiff and sober, try this unbender. Ask them to sit in a circle. The first one says "Ha," the next "Ha, ha," the third "Ha, ha, ha," and so on around the circle with each person adding an extra "Ha." Unless your guests are different from most groups, the crowd will soon be in gales of laughter, and nothing is more contagious than laughter.

BARNYARD SCRAMBLE

Each person is handed a slip of paper with the name of some animal. The number of animals you use depends on the number playing. Each person is to imitate the animal he is and find the others who are making the same noise; thus groups are formed. This is a good mixer and a good way to divide the group into smaller groups.

CIRCLE MIXER

This game is a helpful device in securing partners, threes, fours, teams, or almost any type of grouping.

The players make circles containing as many persons as the signals which are given by the leader. For example, if the leader blows a whistle three times, circles of three would be formed all over the playing space. Any odd players have to come "in the pie"—a space near the leader. After the next signal those in the pie try to get back into some circle. At the close of the playing period, those in the pie may be "It" for the next game.

FIND YOUR TWIN

The leader or host gives each arriving guest a type-written sheet as follows:

Find Your Twin

Time limit—10 minutes

	Yours	Get Auto-graph of Twin
1. Color of Eyes	....	....
2. Favorite hobby	....	....
3. Color of hair	....	....
4. Shoe size	....	....
5. Favorite color	....	....
6. Position held in club (omitted if not a club meeting)		....
7. Favorite food	....	....
8. Number of toes	....	....
9. Favorite drink	....	....
10. Dress or suit size	....	....

Within ten minutes after the starting signal each guest tries to find someone who is his twin in each particular mentioned. For instance, if the player's eyes are blue, he finds another blue-eyed person and asks him to autograph his card opposite item No. 1. Then he hunts a player whose hobby is similar to his for autograph No. 2.

When the closing whistle is blown the one with all ten autograph spaces filled in wins.

INTERVIEW YOUR NEIGHBOR

This game also calls for a typewritten sheet to be handed each guest upon arrival.

Interview Your Neighbor

Name
Place of Birth
Total Years of Experience
Number of Children (or Brothers and Sisters)
Hobbies
Secret Ambition
Summer Activity (or Vacation Plans)
Favorite Animal and Why

At a signal each player turns to his neighbor and fills in his chart. When the whistle is blown charts are exchanged and the record of the guest is read. The most interesting is awarded a prize.

NUTS TO YOU

Give each arriving guest a badge made of construction paper about the size and shape of a big walnut shell. Each shell will bear the name of a nut such as: Wal, Hickory, Beech, Pecan, Hazel, Butter, Brazil, Cashew, Filbert, and Chest. Each guest pins his nut name on himself. This game can be used to divide players into groups. All nuts of one kind can stand together.

AUTOGRAPH

The leader gives each arriving guest a typewritten sheet as follows:

Get the Autograph of the Person Who—

1. Has a rubber band around her wrist ....
2. Is wearing only one earring ....
3. Has a folded handkerchief in one pocket ....
4. Has Scotch tape on his glasses ....
5. Has a string tied around his or her finger ....
6. Is wearing a string of pearls ....
7. Is wearing two belts ....
8. Has a pencil over one ear ....
9. Is wearing a cashmere sweater ....
10. Is wearing two wristwatches ....
11. Has a tack in the bottom of her shoe ....
12. Has red nail polish on her little finger ....
13. Has red hair ....
14. Has a dime in his shoe ....

The player must find someone who qualifies for each of the questions. At the close of ten or fifteen minutes when the whistle is blown, the winner will be the one who has the autograph on all his blank lines.

BAD OMENS

Before the party, type a list of **Bad Omens** or **Superstitions,** one to a card. Then cut each card into several pieces. Scramble them and place several pieces in each envelope. Hand an envelope to each player as he enters. By exchanging pieces with the other players he can get the right pieces to formulate one complete superstition. Here are some familiar superstitions to use:

1. A broken mirror will bring you seven years of bad luck.

2. If you sing before breakfast, you will cry before night.

3. If a black cat crosses your path, you will have bad luck.

4. To walk under a ladder is extremely bad luck.

5. You'll never finish anything started on Friday.

6. If you put on a garment wrong side out, it's bad luck to change.

7. It's bad luck to sneeze before breakfast.

8. It's bad luck to rock an empty chair.

WHITE ELEPHANT

Each player brings a fancily wrapped package containing a white elephant (something around his home of which he is tired). The group is seated in a circle. All the gifts are piled on the floor in the center of the circle.

A couple of dice are started around the circle. The first player to roll a pair takes his choice of the packages. For a large crowd it is livelier to have several pairs of dice in use at the same time.

Each player unwraps his gift and places it in front of him. When the packages from the center have all been taken, then the lucky player walks around the circle inspecting the gifts already opened. He may take his choice. Invariably this leads to lots of good-natured rivalry. Something especially attractive may change hands dozens of times. This is an excellent game in a large group.

GRAND MARCH

One of the best ice breakers and partner choosers is a Grand March. The boys and girls form separate lines on opposite sides of the room, facing the leader. The boys stand at the leader's left, the girls at his right. March music is played or a good marching song can be sung.

1. The lines march forward, then toward each other, the boys passing behind the leader and outside the line of girls while the girls go in front of the leader and inside the line of boys. When the lines meet at the opposite end of the room, the marchers come up the center in twos with arms locked.

2. The first couple goes to the right, the second to the left, the third to the right, and so on, continuing around the room until the lines meet and the marchers come up in fours.

3. The leader divides the fours into couples and again sends the lines around as in 2. When they meet at the other end of the hall, each couple in the left

line joins hands and raises them to form a bridge. The right line passes under the bridges. Both lines continue to march during this figure. When the lines meet at the upper end of the room, the right line forms bridges and the left passes under.

4. When the lines meet at the lower end of the room, the first couple in the left line makes a bridge while the first couple from the right line goes under. The second right couple makes a bridge under which the first couple from the left passes. Thus the couples alternately make bridges or go under them. The figure should be repeated at the other end of the room. This rather difficult step is very popular after the group has become accustomed to marching.

5. At the end of the bridge making, the marchers come up from the lower end of the room in fours with arms locked. The first four go to the right, the second to the left. They return in eights.

6. Each player in the eight takes the hand of his neighbor on each side. The player on the left end of each line looks back of him to the player at the right end of the line behind—whose hand he will presently take. This continues until the whole group is one long winding line, which then is led into a single circle. The serpentine trick leaves each player standing beside the partner with whom he has marched, and these partners can be retained for succeeding games.

DOGGY

Each player is given, upon arrival, an envelope containing paper letters. These letters when placed in the right order spell out a dog's name such as: Rover, Brownie, Scotch, Lassie, etc. As soon as each player figures out his dog's name, he can write it on a slip of paper and pin it on. When a plump "gal" turns out to be "Lassie" and a sober scholar becomes "Soot," it breaks the ice and the party is off to a good start.

SKELETON NAMES

Give each guest a pencil, paper, and a tag. Each player prints his name on the tag in skeleton form. That is, he prints his name, omitting the vowels but marking a dash in place of each vowel omitted. For example, Berniece Thorson would print B-rn--c- Th-rs-n. Each then fastens his tag on himself. Allow about ten minutes for everyone to go about the room and from the skeleton names write down as many names as possible. The person getting the most names in a given time wins. If the crowd is well acquainted, have the players choose and wear names of actors, authors, or musicians.

PAPER BAG HANDSHAKE

Players are given a good sized paper bag and pencil. The bag is put on one hand (not the one used for writing) and the player goes about interviewing other players. He writes the names, addresses and other interesting facts about those with whom he talks until the bag is covered with writing.

FIVE PENNIES

Secretly give one penny to each of the first five guests to arrive. Ask them to say nothing about the coins. When all guests are present, explain that everyone must shake hands with everyone else. If a person shakes hands with one having the coin, the coin is passed with the shaking of the hand and continues to be passed until the whistle is blown. The ones who hold the coins when the whistle is blown may keep them.

GATHERING NUTS

The leader moves about and selects a player taking him by the hand and leading him among other players. This player takes another person as they move about. Each new player takes someone from the crowd until a fairly long line is following the leader. Leader lines them up and solemnly announces, "This is The Gathering of the Nuts."

2.

Single-Circle Games

The very shy and very conservative, who wouldn't think of doing an individual stunt, forget themselves when they gather in a circle for a game. There's something about rubbing elbows with the next player to develop a friendly spirit. For the more aggressive there's plenty of opportunity for individual performance in many circle games.

The single circle is the simplest formation to get a group into quickly. The leader, taking the hands of two players, asks the group to join hands and form a circle. For a very large group, two or more separate circles should be formed.

NUMBER CALL

The players number themselves around the circle, leaving one player in the center. "It" in the center of the circle calls out two numbers. The persons whose numbers are called must change places. "It" tries to get one of the places vacated. The person who is left without a place becomes "It." This may be played with the players seated or standing.

SLAP TAG

All players stand in a circle, clasping hands. "It" runs around outside the circle tagging another player as he runs. The one tagged immediately runs around the outside of the circle in the opposite direction. The object of each runner is to get back first to the vacant place. The successful runner remains in the place he won, and the unsuccessful one becomes "It."

ORIENTAL TAG

This is a variation of **Slap Tag**. All players stand in a circle. "It" runs around outside the circle, tagging another player as he runs. The one tagged immediately runs around the outside of the circle in the opposite direction, but he places one hand wherever he was tagged. If he was tagged on his ankle, he places one hand on his ankle as he tries to tag "It." The object of each runner is to get back first to the vacant place. The successful runner remains in the place he won, and the unsuccessful one becomes "It."

CIRCLE TAG

Circle tag calls for the players to stand in a spread-out circle equidistant from each other. At a signal, all run clockwise around the circle. Each player tries to tag the player in front of him. When a player is tagged, he drops out of the game, standing in the center of the circle where he awaits the finish of the game with other players who have been tagged. The last player in the chase is the winner.

JUMP THE SHOT

Players form a circle sufficiently large so that each will be free to jump. "Swinger" stands in the center of the circle. He has a rope at least as long as the radius of the circle with a knotted towel tied on the free end of the rope to weight that end.

The Swinger starts swinging the weight on a short radius, paying out the rope as he increases speed so that by the time the object at the end of the rope reaches the players on the circle, it will be in steady motion close to the floor. The players jump the rope as it passes them. A player cannot step off the circle to avoid jumping. When a player misses he drops out of the game until a second player misses. The first player then returns to the circle. This is a strenuous game. Play for a limited time.

BRONCO

This is a game especially enjoyed by boys. One player is the bronco who stands in a circle formed by players who have their hands joined. The players try to prevent the bronco from breaking through the circle. He may break through by crawling under or over joined hands, or by breaking the hand-holds of the players. Whenever he breaks through, the players chase him to tag him. The boy who first tags the bronco becomes Bronco for the next game.

TWO DEEP

The players, except two, stand in a circle facing the center of the circle. One of the two players is runner, the other is the chaser who tries to catch the runner as he runs around the circle. The runner saves himself from being tagged by stepping in front of one of the players in the circle; that player immediately becomes the runner and the chaser tries to tag him. Whenever the chaser tags the runner, the runner becomes the chaser and the game continues.

LEAPFROG TWO DEEP

This game is a variation of plain Two Deep. The players, except two, stand in leapfrog position in the circle, facing the center. The runner may leap over any player, but when he stops in front of him that player must then run. Whenever the chaser tags the runner, they exchange positions. Frequently the runners have a tendency to keep going too long before stopping in front of anyone. It is well to explain that skillful players leap over several people and then suddenly stop.

GOSSIP

The first person in the circle whispers an observation to his right-hand neighbor. The recipient whispers it to his neighbor, and the message goes around the group. No whisper can be repeated and each player passes on what he hears. When the remark reaches the last person he repeats it aloud and the leader repeats what he actually said.

LOST LOVER

This is a game enjoyed by teen-agers. Players are seated in a circle with "It" blindfolded in the center.

"It" gropes about in search of a lap, sits down, and says to the victim, "Are you my lost lover?" Victim answers in a disguised voice. He can groan, bark like a dog, meow like a cat, etc., while "It" tries to recognize who he is. One guess is allowed. If it is correct, "It" takes the chair and the victim takes "Its" place. If not, "It" finds another lap.

POORHOUSE

The players are seated in chairs arranged in groups of two around a large semi-circle. Facing the semi-circle are two chairs known as the "Poorhouse." The couples in the semi-circle count off 1, 2, 3, etc., so that each couple has a number. The couple who is "It" call two or three numbers. The couples whose numbers have been called must quickly change places before the couple in the "Poorhouse" moves into one of their houses. The couple left without chairs is automatically in the "Poorhouse." If a couple lets go hands at any time, they are automatically in the "Poorhouse" also.

BEEP BEEP

The players are arranged in little circles of three all about the room. The leader calls directions such as "traffic to the right," at which term the little circles turn to the right and keep turning until the leader says "traffic to the left," when they quickly shift and turn around to the left. When the leader says "Beep beep," all the players must quickly form a new circle with two other people. At this time the leader steps in and becomes one of the circles. The one left over is the new leader.

HEAD NUT

Give the players several walnuts or peanuts to pass around the circle. The person in the center is called "Head Nut." He tries to find out where the nuts are. If he stops the person who holds a nut at the moment, that person becomes Head Nut, and the first Head Nut gets all the nuts being passed at the time. If he misses, whoever holds a nut pockets it, and new nuts are started. The one who captures the most nuts at the end of the game is the winner.

CATCH THE CANE

Ten to thirty or more players stand in a circle and number consecutively. One player stands in the center of the circle holding with his index finger a cane, yardstick or closed umbrella, which stands perpendicular to the floor. Suddenly he lifts his finger from the cane, at the same time calling the number assigned to one of the players in the circle. The person whose number is called must run forward and catch the cane before it lies on the floor. If he fails, he returns to his place in the circle. If successful, he changes places with the center player.

RING RING

A finger ring is slipped onto a long string. Players form a circle holding onto the string which is tied together at the ends. Players pass the ring from one to another by sliding their hands back and forth on the string. "It," the player in the center, tries to guess who has the ring. He may stop its passing at any time to make a player lift his hands. If the player has the ring, he becomes "It." If not, the game continues until "It" discovers who has the ring.

WHO IS THE LEADER?

Players stand or sit in a circle. One player goes out. A leader starts some action such as clapping and the group does it until the player returns to the center. The leader then changes the action and the player tries to discover who the leader is. Be careful that all of the players do not watch the leader. When the leader is spotted he goes out of the room, and the game starts again.

CHESHIRE GRIN

Players, who are now Halloween cats, form a circle. All cats are sober until the leader points at one. That cat grins like a Cheshire, wipes the grin off and throws it across the circle to a friend. The friend grabs the grin, spreads it on his face and smiles broadly. Players toss the grin back and forth. If a player smiles out of turn, he's out. The ousted cats leer to make players laugh. The last three sober-sides win awards.

PASS THE SHOE

Players are seated in a circle. Each removes one shoe and places it in front of him. At a signal each person moves a shoe to his right to the song of "We will pass the shoe from me to you, to you, We will pass the shoe and do just as I do." On the word "do," each player takes the shoe in front of him and taps it on the right side; on the words "just as," he taps the shoe on the left; and on the words "I do" he taps the shoe in the center. If a person ends up without a shoe, he is eliminated.

STACK-'EM

Players are divided into two circles. Each player is given a match. A milk bottle is placed a few paces in front of the group. The object is to see which group can first stack all its matches on the bottle.

HAVE YOU SEEN MY SHEEP?

One player, who is the shepherd, stands outside the circle. He taps on someone's back and says, "Good morning." The tapped player, who is a housekeeper, replies, "Good morning." The shepherd says, "Have you seen my sheep?" The housekeeper asks, "What does he look like?" The shepherd then describes a player near the housekeeper. He may say, "Oh, he has a blue tie, a brown coat, tan shoes," etc. As soon as the sheep recognizes itself or the housekeeper knows who is being described, both begin to run outside the circle, the housekeeper trying to catch the sheep before it gets back to its place in the circle. If this happens the sheep must go into the center, which is called "in the soup," where he remains until the end of the game. Whether or not the sheep is caught, the housekeeper becomes the shepherd for the next time. The shepherd does no chasing. When he has described his sheep, he steps into the housekeeper's place.

SHOUT THE NUMBER

The players may stand or be seated. All the players take consecutive numbers. One player takes his place in the center of the circle and calls two numbers as "Four and Seven." The persons whose numbers are called must change places. While they do so, the center player tries to get one of their places. The person who is left without a place becomes the center player. After a time "It" may call more than two numbers.

BLINDFOLD NUMBER CHANGE

(A variation of **Shout the Number**) Blindfold "It" and permit him to either tag a player or get into a vacated place after two or more numbers are called. The players whose numbers are called move quietly and stealthily.

If the players are seated on chairs, "It" may call "Stormy weather!" occasionally which means that all players must change places.

LOST MIDGET

For this game use a small stuffed doll or knot a handkerchief to look like a man. Choose one child to be "It," and have the rest of the children stand in a circle around him. The object of the game is for "It" to try to catch the "midget" while the players in the circle toss it from one to the other. If "It" succeeds, the one who tossed it last has to be "It," while the other takes his place.

SQUIRRELS IN TREES

All the players but two form small circles of four with hands joined. Each group numbers off 1-2-3-4. Number 1 of each circle steps inside and is a squirrel. The other three players with hands joined around him are a hollow tree. The trees should scatter so that they are a fair distance from each other.

One of the extra players is a homeless squirrel (It) and the other is a fox or hound (the chaser). The fox tries to catch the homeless squirrel. The squirrel may escape by running under the arms of the players into one of the trees. As there can be only one squirrel in a tree at a time, the squirrel already there must get out and run to another tree, being chased by the fox.

If the fox catches any squirrel in the open, that squirrel becomes the fox and turns around to chase the other one.

After a time the leader asks the number twos in the circles to become squirrels—a little later the threes and fours. In this way all players take turns being squirrels.

RHYTHM

Players are seated in a circle. They number off. Everyone taps on the knees twice, claps hands twice, and snaps the fingers of his right hand. One person starts by calling his own number on the first snap and another person's number on the second snap. The person whose number is called must repeat his own number on the next snap and call someone else's number on the following snap. A person who breaks the rhythm is eliminated.

RABBIT

All players are instructed to form a circle and stoop down. One person says to the next, "Do you know how to play 'Rabbit?' " A player says "No," and asks the next player. So on around the circle until everyone has responded in the negative. Starter then says, "Well, then what are we all doing in this silly position?"

WAISTLINE

This game is especially good for teen-agers or adults. All players stand in a circle. Each is given a length of string and asked to make a circle with it, the size of his or her own waistline. Most people make too big a circle. The leader with a tape line then measures the circle and the waistline of the owner. The one whose circle of string most correctly corresponds with the waist measurement wins. This game creates much hilarity.

MATCH-BOTTLE

Players are each given fifteen matches (kitchen variety). A milk bottle is passed around the circle. Each player puts one match on the mouth of the bottle. The player who spills the pile of matches must keep all the matches he drops and start over. The object of the game is to see who can get rid of his matches first.

CHINESE PUZZLE

The group is divided into smaller groups of about ten each, who form small circles around the room. Each group sends one of their members out of the room, then selects a leader who will wind and twist up the circle until it is tightly intertwined. The whole group must keep hold of hands during this process. The person coming back must find out the leader responsible for the twisting, and then untwist the group without breaking handholds.

SNIP

A player points or tosses a knotted handkerchief at one of the circle, then pronounces and spells a three-letter word, as "Now, N-O-W." Then he immediately counts to twelve and says "Snip." Before he reaches "Snip," the person to whom he pointed must name three objects, the first beginning with N, the second with O, and the third with W, as "nuts, out, white." If he does not finish in time, he becomes the next "IT."

CALF IN CORRAL

Players form a circle with one player, a cowboy, outside of circle. Cowboy taps one of the players on the back and says, "Good morning." The player answers "Good morning." The cowboy says, "Have you seen my calf?" The player asks, "How is it dressed?" The cowboy then describes a player in the circle as his calf. As soon as the calf recognizes himself or the player knows who is being described, both begin to run outside the circle, the player trying to catch the calf before it gets back to its place in the circle. If caught, the calf goes into the corral in the center of the circle where he remains until the end of the game. At any rate, the chaser becomes the new cowboy.

TEAKETTLE

Send one player from the room. The group decides on some homonymns (words that sound alike but have different meanings) such as:

1. rain, reign, rein	11. by, bye, buy
2. bare, bear (to carry) bear (an animal)	12. raise, rays, raze
	13. pole, poll
3. in, inn	14. tail, tale
4. pane, pain	15. rose, rows
5. sore, soar	16. vein, vane
6. fare, fair	17. pale, pail
7. dear, deer	18. bow, bough, beau
8. so, sow, sew	19. bawl, ball
9. plain, plane	20. do, due, dew
10. piece, peace	

When the player returns, each person in the room greets him with a sentence using the word, "Teakettle," in place of the selected word. One may say, "I grabbed the teakettle (rein);" another, "His was a very short teakettle (reign);" a third, "Did you go through the teakettle (rain)?" The player whose sentence reveals the "teakettle" word becomes "It" and leaves the room for the next game.

Variations: Have "It" ask each player a question. The answer must contain the selected word using the word "teakettle" to hide it.

Allow the players to ask the absent one the questions using "teakettle" instead of the word selected.

Have the absent player think of a pair of homonyms using them in a sentence, supplying the word "teakettle" rather than saying the word itself. The others try to guess the words the leader has in mind.

BUZZ

One of the players starts the game by saying "One;" the others in turn say, "Two," "Three," "Four," "Five," and "Six." But when the number seven is reached that player must say "Buzz." The next player says "Eight" and so on around but "Buzz" is used instead of any multiple of seven (as 14, 21, 28) and instead of any number containing seven (as 17 and 27). For 71 the players say "Buzz one," and for 72 "Buzz two" and so on; and for 77 "Buzz, buzz." If a player says a number when he should say "Buzz" or says "Buzz" in the wrong place, he is out of the game and must be silent. The counting is continued at once by the next player. If a player forgets his number or miscounts after a Buzz, he must pay a forfeit, but can continue playing. The object of the game is to reach one hundred. If the counting is carried on quickly, the game will be found to be a lively one.

Variations: Add the word "Fizz," using it for five and multiples of five. Or let the starter select what the "Buzz" number is to be when the game starts over again.

MUSICAL MARCH

Players form a circle and each is given a book. Each player balances a book on his head and marches to music. When the music stops each player kneels on the floor and remains in that position until the music begins again. If the book falls to the floor or is touched by the hand of the player, that player is disqualified and withdraws. The game continues until only one player is left.

JINGLE BELL

The players stand in a circle with their hands behind them. One player is given the bell. A leader is chosen to stand in the center of the circle and close his eyes—or be blindfolded. He then counts slowly to ten, the counts coming about a second apart. Upon the first count, whoever has the bell rings it vigorously, and then takes the clapper in his hand and passes it behind his back to the neighbor either to the right or left. On the count of ten, the movements stop and the leader opens his eyes. He guesses who has the bell. Anyone caught with the bell becomes the next leader.

HAT PUSH

Equipment: cowboy or other wide-brimmed hat.

Players clasp hands and form a circle. Hat is placed

in the center on its crown. The players, keeping their hands clasped, try to pull and push each other so as to make someone knock the hat over. Each player who bumps the hat over drops out of the circle. The hat is righted and the game continues until a single winner remains.

COMPLIMENTS

This is a good game for a girls' party. All but one player forms a circle. That one player leaves the room. While she is gone someone pays her a compliment. Upon her return to the room the leader says, "Someone has paid you a compliment. Who was it?" The girl has three guesses to learn the identity of her admirer. If she guesses correctly, that one leaves the room. If she doesn't guess her admirer, she chooses someone else to leave.

MY HORSE

Players are seated in a circle. The first player says, "My horse is active." The next player to his right repeats the sentence, adding an adjective beginning with "B." For instance, "My horse is active and bony." The third might say, "My horse is active, bony, and clever." And so on around the circle. Anyone not able to think of an adjective beginning with the next letter of the alphabet drops out of the circle, or if a player can't repeat the adjectives given, he drops out of the game.

RHYTHM OF NOUNS

Players are all seated in a circle. The leader starts a three-beat rhythm and everyone joins in. On the count of one, hands are clapped on knees; on the count of two, hands are clapped together in front; and on the three all snap their fingers with arms outstretched parallel to their shoulders. At the count of three the leader names a common noun such as "elephant." Without breaking the one, two, three rhythm, the player next gives a noun beginning with the last letter of the word "elephant" such as "teacher" beginning with "T." The noun must be given on the third beat of the rhythm. The one who can't think of a noun quickly enough drops out of the game until the winner is finally determined.

CIRCUS

The players are seated in a circle. The first one says, "I went to the circus to see an anteater." The next in line repeats, "I went to the circus to see an anteater," and adds an animal whose name begins with the letter "B" such as "Bear." The third in line might say, "I went to the circus and saw an anteater, a bear, and a cheetah." One who fails to think of an animal beginning with the next letter of the alphabet goes to the center of the circle.

ALPHABET FACE

The players are seated in a circle. The first player turns to the one on his right and says, "You have a face" to which the other replies, "What kind of face?" The first player then must answer with a descriptive adjective beginning with "A." He could say, "You have an angelic face," or "an attractive face," or if he feels funny he might say, "You have an awful face." The next player turns to the one on his right and says, "You have a face." The second player answers the inquiry, "What kind of a face?" with an adjective beginning with "B" and so on around the circle and through the alphabet. The same adjective cannot be used twice. Anyone who can't think of an adjective beginning with the right letter before the leader counts to ten must leave the circle and sit in the center while the others finish the game. The game gets very exciting towards the close when only two or three of the sharpest are left to seek new adjectives.

BUMPITY, BUMP, BUMP

Players gather in a circle. The leader stands in the center and starts the game off. He walks up to some person unexpectedly and with his hands at his ears, flapping them like a donkey's, says very rapidly, "Bumpity, bump, bump, bump." The person before whom he stands is supposed to count five before he finishes. If he fails to do so, he takes the place in the center of the circle and the leader takes his place and the game continues.

DINNER

All players sit in a circle. Each person names an article of food beginning with a letter found in the word "Dinner." The first could be "duck," the second "ice cream," etc. The word "Dinner" can be used as many times around the circle as desired. Of course, the longer the game is played the harder it becomes because names of foods can't be repeated. When some-one fails to think of an article of food he drops out of the game. Gradually all but one will be eliminated and he'll be the winner.

WINKUM

This is an old game but still a favorite. The girls are seated in chairs facing a circle. There is one empty chair. Behind every chair stands a boy. All boys stand stiffly with their hands at their sides. The boy behind the empty chair becomes "It" and must get a girl to fill his chair. When he sees a girl he'd like to have sit in his chair, he winks at her.

She must slip away from her chair before the boy at her back can restrain her by putting his hands on her shoulders. If she escapes, her boy becomes "It" and must fill his chair. If she doesn't escape, "It" must try to get another girl for his chair.

RHYMES

The players stand or sit in a circle with one in the center. The center player says a word of one syllable, and points to someone in the circle who must give a word that rhymes with it before the one in the center counts to ten. Should he fail to do this he must change places with the center player. If he succeeds the one in the center must repeat the play.

HOW DO YOU LIKE YOUR NEIGHBOR?

Players sit in a circle. The center player goes up to any player and asks, "How do you like your neighbor?" He may answer, "Very well." If he does all the players must exchange seats. If he answers, "Not at all," the questioner asks "Whom would you rather have?" He answers, "No. 5 and 11" (or any number he chooses). These two numbers named must change seats with the two who sit on either side of the person who names them. The questioner tries to get any one of the four seats.

CROSSED WIRES

All players sit in a circle with the leader in the center. The leader says: "With your right hand grab your left ear. Now with your left hand grab your nose." When each has hold of his ear and nose, the leader calls, "Change." The difficulty encountered in reversing is always amusing. Such stunts start laughter and serve to break the formality of the group.

3·

Double-Circle Games

In double-circle games, the players form two circles, one inside the other. If the number of players is large, they may form two or more double circles.

CHIT CHAT

Players form a double circle, boys in the outer circle, girls in the inner. When the music starts, the circles move in opposite directions. When the music stops, or at the leader's signal, the players stop, face each other, and chat with the person facing him. When the music starts, the circles march as before. The leader should call frequent, brief stops. It is fun to suggest a topic to chat about for each stop.

WASHINGTON FRUIT BASKET

The players pair off in couples and all but one couple seat themselves around the room. The remaining couple become George and Martha Washington. Each of the seated couples secretly decide on a fruit to be their name. George and Martha wander around the room calling out the names of various fruits such as cherries, apples, and pears. If a couple's fruit name is called they leave their chairs and follow after George and Martha. If George and Martha call out, "The fruit trees are all in bloom," everyone leaves his seat and follows the Washingtons. When George calls, "The fruit is all ripe," everyone dashes for a chair. The two not getting chairs become George and Martha for the next try.

FIRE IN THE MOUNTAIN

All players except one form a double-circle facing inward, each in the outer circle standing directly behind his partner. The extra player, "It," stands in the center. When he calls "Fire in the Mountain! Run, boys, run!" the players in the outside circle begin at once to jog around to the right while "It" and the players on the inside circle clap their hands and stamp their feet. When "It" stops clapping and holds his hands high over his head, the players in the inside circle do likewise. This is a signal that the outside players are each to try to get in front of an inside player. "It" tries to do the same, and the player left out becomes "It" for the next time.

FACE TO FACE

Partners stand facing each other in one large circle. One player, "It," stands in the center and calls "Face to face," "Back to back," the players taking their positions accordingly. When he calls "Change," all players take new partners. "It" tries to get one too. If he suc-. ceeds, the person left without a partner goes into the center and gives commands.

Variation: The calls may be varied with "Elbows to elbows," "Right foot to right foot," "Left shoulder to left shoulder," and so on.

ONE, TWO, THREE, CHANGE

This is a variation of "Face to Face" and should not be used in the same program with it. The partners stand back to back with elbows hooked together. An extra player who is "It" stands in the center and calls, "One, two, three, change!" "It" grabs a partner, and so does everyone else except one leftover, who becomes "It" for the next time. No pair is safe until both elbows are locked together.

COUPLE TAG

Couples link arms and place outside hands at their waist. All face the same direction in a double circle. A chaser and runner weave in and out among the couples. The runner can save himself by linking arms with either player of any couple. The other player of the couple becomes the runner, and must leave at once. If the runner is tagged, he becomes the chaser. The fun comes when runners link arms often.

THREE DEEP

Each player in the outer circle stands directly be-hind a player in the inner circle and all face toward the center. Two extra players, one of whom is runner and the other chaser, start outside the circle, generally on opposite sides. The object of the game is for the chaser to tag the runner. The runner may save himself by entering the circle and stopping in front of any couple. Thereupon, that file having been made three deep, the outer player, or "Third man," can be tagged, so that he becomes the runner.

In the same way he may save himself from the chaser by stopping in front of a couple. If the chaser tags the runner, they exchange places, the runner becoming chaser and the chaser becoming the runner. Although both runner and chaser may dash through the circle, they may not pause within it except as the runner stops in front of a couple. If they confuse the play by hesitating while running through, the privilege of running through may be withdrawn, all chasing being confined to the outside of the circle.

PARTNER STOOP

Partners first form a double circle. The leader reminds each person to remember his partner. When the music starts or the group sings a lively song, the inner circle marches in one direction and the outer circle marches in the opposite. When the whistle blows, the partners run to each other, join both hands and stoop or squat down. The last couple "down" goes "in the soup" to act as judges for the next round. Partners try to stay out of "the soup" as long as possible.

THIRD MAN

The game "Third Man" is a variation of "Three Deep." After getting into a circular formation the players scatter irregularly about in couples. The players in each couple stand facing each other, clasping hands, with the distance of a long step between them. To make a success of the game the couples should be a considerable distance apart.

Of the two odd players, one is the runner and the other the chaser, as in "Three Deep." The runner may take refuge between any two players who are standing as a couple. The moment that he does so, the one toward whom his back is turned becomes "third man" and must try to avoid being tagged by the chaser.

FLYING DUTCHMAN

Players form a ring by couples. Couples hold hands. One couple stands outside the circle and holds hands as they start around it. Directly they split hands of some couple in the circle and run around the circle and continue running around the circle. The couple touched starts running immediately in the opposite direction, holding hands as they run. The first couple back to the vacancy remains in the circle and the other couple is "It."

Variation: When running couples meet the boys shake hands and the girls bow and say "Howdy."

ARCH

All players join hands in a single circle. A couple forms an arch over the circle at each end of the playing space. When the music starts or the group sings, the players march around under the arches. At a signal the two arches come down, trying to catch someone. Those caught go "in the soup" and stay there until a partner comes who has been caught elsewhere. These partners then form other arches about the circle. Continue until all are caught and there is a circle of arches.

YANKEE DOODLE

The group forms a double circle, the girls in the outside circle, the boys on the inside. While Yankee Doodle is sung the partners walk around the circle.

> Father and I went down to camp,
>   Along with Captain Goodwin,
> And there we saw the men and boys
>   As thick as hasty pudding.

> #### Chorus
> Yankee Doodle, keep it up,
>   Yankee Doodle, dandy;
> Mind the music and the step
>   And with the girls be handy.

During "Yankee Doodle, keep it up" the partners join hands and slide four steps in the direction they have been marching. They slide back during "Yankee Doodle, dandy." Each couple swings around with six steps during "Mind the music and the step." Then each boy moves to the girl on his left and bows during "With the girls be handy." The game is repeated with these new partners.

4.

Relays

Competition is the spice of life, so we are told. We are not sure about its place in life, but we do know that competition is the spice needed to enliven every party, or social gathering. For it's a dull party that keeps guests in their chairs all evening. A lively relay will make your guests scramble around a little till they may be short of breath but we'll warrant they'll be long on enthusiasm.

Relay races may be played by two or more teams with an equal number of players in each team. Usually the players stand in single file, the first in each team toeing the starting line.

WATERMELON RACE

Cut a watermelon into quarters. Place the four pieces of watermelon lengthwise at the edge of a kitchen table. At the far end of each watermelon put an empty glass. If this is a teen-age group choose two boys and two girls to enter the race. Tie their hands behind their backs. The contestant who can place the most watermelon seeds in the glass in five minutes wins.

COTTON BOWL RELAY

Set two large punch bowls on two small tables. Sprinkle around the empty bowls small balls of cotton. (Boxes of cotton balls can be bought in any drug or dime store.) Divide the players into two teams. Blindfold the first two players. Hand each a large wooden spoon. At a signal ask each one to spoon into the bowl as many cotton balls as he can in two minutes. Inasmuch as the balls have no weight, the blindfolded dipper cannot tell whether he is scooping balls or missing them. It is hilarious to watch. When the first two players are through, count the number of balls in each bowl. Let each member of the teams compete. Add the totals at the completion of the game. The team getting the most balls in the bowl is the winner.

(Variation for Washington's birthday party: turn the cotton balls into red cherries with vegetable coloring.)

RING SPEAR

Divide the group into two teams. Hang two curtain rings head high in an open doorway. Line up the teams ten feet from the rings. Give the first player of each team a pair of opera glasses. He focuses the glasses on the ring, walks to it, and without hesitation reaches up and puts his finger through the ring. One trial is all he gets. Action must be quick. Then he returns to the next in line and gives him the opera glasses. The score-keeper keeps score on who gets a finger in the ring. The team who makes the most successful jabs wins.

FROGMEN

This, too, is a relay to be played by two teams. The first player of each team pulls on a burlap bag over his feet and holds it up with his hands. He hops across the room and back again. He then hands his bag to the next in line. The team finishing first wins.

BUTTON SNAP

Divide the group into two or more teams, depending on the number of players. Line the teams up single file on one side of the room. Set a goal across the room. Mark a starting line. Give the leader of each line two smooth, medium-size buttons. One he places on the starting line. With the other he snaps the first button to the goal. "Snapping" consists of pressing the edge of one button with the other in such a way that the under one flies ahead. As soon as the players reach the goal they race back and hand the buttons to the second player in line. The line finishing first wins the relay.

SHOE BOX RELAY

For this game you need four shoe boxes. (It is good to have a spare or two in case one is broken.) The group divides into two teams of equal number. At a given signal the first one in each line puts a shoe box on

each foot and tries to run across the space to the opposite line and back. The second one in line is all ready
when the first one returns to put on the boxes and try
his speed. The line which can finish first is the winning team.

PAPER RELAY

The first player in each line is given two pieces of
cardboard about eight by ten inches. The player steps
on one piece of cardboard with his left foot and places
the other piece as far ahead as he can easily step with
his right foot. Standing on his right foot, he picks up
the cardboard from under his left foot and advances
it ahead of the right foot. The object of the game is to
walk across the room and back, stepping on the paper
all the way. In other words, the player lays his own
stepping stones as he goes. The team finishing first
wins.

NECKTIE RELAY

The first player in each line is given a necktie or a
large cotton handkerchief. At a signal from the whistle, he ties the necktie or handkerchief onto the neck
of the player behind. As soon as the bow is tied, the second player unties it, turns, and ties it on the third player. The team that first reaches the last player at the
end of the line wins the game.

TRANSFER RELAY

The first two players in each team join hands.
When the whistle blows they run to the goal line. The

first player stays there while the second player runs back to join hands with the third player. These two run to the goal line and the second player remains while the third returns for the fourth. The team that first transfers all its members to the goal line wins the race.

BUNDLE RELAY

The object of this relay is for each line to try to tie themselves into a bundle before the opposing team does. The first player in each line is given a ball of cord. At a signal he passes it to the next in line behind him, but holds the end. The ball is passed from player to player, unrolling as it goes. When it arrives at the end of the line it is passed up the line behind the backs of the players until it reaches the first player again. The team that first wraps itself into a bundle is the winner. The sequel to the race consists in untying the bundle by passing the ball back and winding it as it goes.

TURN ABOUT RELAY

This relay is as much fun to watch as to play. Each team can have as many players as are available, but actually needs only two or three members. The players stand at the base line. When the whistle is blown each first player runs toward the goal line until it is blown again. Then he must turn, if he has not reached the goal, and run back toward the base line. Each time the whistle sounds the runners change their direction. When the player finally reaches the goal line and returns to the base line, he touches off the next player in his line.

HANDFUL RELAY

The first player in each team is given fifteen clothespins or sticks. At the starting signal he puts all of them on the floor in front of the person behind him. This player must pick them up and lay them before the next person in line. Each player must have all the clothespins or other objects in his hands when he passes them. The team that finishes first wins the relay.

OVER AND UNDER

The first player in each team is given a ball, or bean bag. At the starting signal he passes the ball over his head to the second player, who passes it between his knees to the third, who hands it over his head to the fourth. Thus the ball goes alternately overhead and between knees to the last player who runs to the head of the line and starts it back over his head. The game proceeds until a line has regained its original order, with the first player at the head again. The line finishing first wins the race.

BLACKBOARD RELAY

Two teams line up in front of a blackboard. The first player in each line is given a piece of chalk. When the whistle is blown the first player walks to the board, writes a word, returns to his line, and gives the chalk to the second player. This is repeated until the end of the line is reached, each player adding a word to the sentence the first player started. The team that first finishes a complete and intelligible sentence in which each player has written a word wins.

ELECTRIC SHOCK

The players in each team stand side by side with hands joined, one team facing another. When the whistle blows, the first player presses the hand of the second, the second then presses the hand of the third, and so on down the line. (This also may be played by the first in line lightly tapping the shoulder of the second in line, etc., to the end of the line.) The team first reaching the end of the line wins.

HEEL DUSTING

The first player in each team has a scarf in his right hand. On the starting signal, he reaches between his knees and places the scarf against the left heel of the player behind. The next player may not stoop until his heel is "dusted."

WASHDAY RELAY

The first player of each line is given two scarves and three clothespins. At the signal, player number one of each line runs to a clothesline, hangs his wash, and returns to the end of the line. The next player runs up, takes down the laundry, gives it to the third person in line who hangs it, and so on to the end of the team. The line finishing first is the winner.

PEBBLE PASS

Teams stand in two lines facing each other. Five pebbles are placed on the floor at the head of each line. Each player weaves his fingers into the fingers of his neighbor. They must not unclasp hands throughout the game. At a signal player number one picks up the pebbles one at a time and passes them down the line, the last player puts them on the floor beside him. If a pebble is dropped, it must be picked up without any unclasping of hands.

Variations: (1) Have the players clasp their hands behind them. (2) Have the players cross their arms before weaving the fingers together.

ROPE SKIPPING RELAY

On the signal the first player in each line jumps rope in the usual way to the goal about twenty-five feet away and returns. He gives the rope to the second in line who does likewise. Continue until all have completed the skipping. The line finishing first wins.

HOOP RELAY

At the signal "go" the first player passes a hoop or loop of rope over his head, around the body and to the ground, steps out and hands it to the next player who does the same thing. The team finishing first wins.

TIN CAN RELAY

An object or a goal line is placed twenty-five feet in front of each line. At a signal the first player kicks the can down around the object and back to the next player on his team. Allow players to move up to the starting line but not beyond it until the can is kicked back. Continue until all the players complete the action.

SIR WALTER RALEIGH

Relay is done in couples. The lady stands on two pieces of paper. The lady cannot progress except as she steps on the papers. The man advances the papers for her to step on. When the first couple reaches the goal and returns, the second couple in line starts off. The line finishing first wins.

CORK WHISK RELAY

A cork is placed on the floor before each line and the first player in each line is given a whiskbroom. (A heavy paper folded and a string tied about one end for a handle will serve as a whisk.) A goal is established about ten feet in front of the lines. On a starting signal the player begins brushing the cork to the goal and back. Upon the return he gives the whiskbroom to the second player and goes to the end of the line. The play continues until all have arrived home safely.

TOUCH AND GO

The players form in lines of five or six and each line acts as a unit. The leader names something in sight. This may be as indefinite as wood, iron, or water; or it may be a specific object, as the garage door, a certain tree, or a player (who tries to run away from the rest). The leader may give directions, as "Hop back on the right foot." The first player in each line sets out to touch the object and return to his place. Then the second player takes his turn. The line first regaining its original position wins the race.

HIGH, WIDE AND HANDSOME

The players are divided into two teams. In front of each line put newspapers on the floor a good step apart. Give the first player of each team a book to balance on his head as he walks across the room and back on the newspapers. On his return the next one starts. The team finishing first wins the race.

GO AND GO BACK

This relay race is especially good for picnic programs because it is fun to watch. Each team need have only two or three members. The players stand at the base line. At a whistle signal each first player runs toward the goal line until the whistle is blown again. If he has not reached the goal, he must turn and run back toward the base line. Each time the whistle sounds the runners change their direction. The race may finish at the goal line or at the base line. If it ends at the goal, the player must dash back to touch off the next player in his line.

ANIMAL RELAY

This relay is especially good for younger children. Assign a different animal to each member of the team such as donkey, crab, lame dog, bear, etc. Give a like animal to the opposing member of the other team. At a signal, the first donkeys travel on all fours to the goal, imitating the donkey's kick and bray; the crab walks on all fours with face up; a lame dog walks on two hands and one foot; a bear walks on all fours with feet going outside of hands; a duck walks on two feet in a squat position. The team finishing first wins the relay.

SPIDER RELAY

The group is divided into two teams of an equal number of couples. Each couple stands back to back, locking their arms together. At a signal the front couple runs for a designated goal. Running toward the goal the man is running forward and the girl backward. Returning, the opposite is true, the girl runs forward and the man backward. The team finishing first wins.

BALLOON RELAY

For this relay the boys compete with the girls. Each contestant is given a balloon. When the race starts, the first one in line runs down to the end of the room where a chair is placed, blows up his balloon, then sits on the balloon until it bursts. He then runs back to tag the next person in his line. Caution: It is unfair for contestants to inflate their balloons before reaching the chair.

Variation: Inflated balloons can be handed each contestant as he leaves the starting mark. After burst-

ing his balloon by sitting on it, he returns to tag the
next in line.

CHINS DOWN

Did you ever try to pass an orange from under your
chin to under his? It's a neck-tickling game and an up-
roarious one. Line up the players in two teams—each
team alternating boy, girl, boy, girl. Hand the captain
of each team an orange. Instruct him to put it under his
chin and hold it there. Without using his hands he must
pass it to the next in line. No one may use his hands,
except to pick it off the floor when it falls. This game
is hilarious as Mr. Tall tries to pass it "chinwise" to
Miss Short. The first group through wins.

NAME SPELLDOWN

The girls challenge the boys to a "Name spelling
contest." Boys line up opposite the girls. The first girl
must spell a boy's name beginning with the last letter
of the name of the boy across from her, before the captain counts to ten. Then the boy must spell a girl's
name beginning with the last letter of the name just
spelled.

For instance, Tom and Mary are the first couple.
Mary spells a boy's name beginning with "M," the last
letter in Tom's name, before the count of ten. If she
chooses "Manuel," Tom must then spell a girl's name
of his own choosing beginning with the letter "L," such
as Lucile, Lillian, or Lois. The turn then goes to the
next girl in line.

When a player fails to think of a name or spells it incorrectly before the count of ten he drops out. The last speller selects another name to give to the next member of the opposing team.

The game may be played until only one player is left.

PEANUT EATING

The group is divided into couples. Each couple is given ten unshelled peanuts. The object is for one of the couple to shell the peanuts and feed them to the other member of the couple. The couple through first wins. If the group is too large, eight or ten couples may be chosen to perform the stunt for the amusement of the others.

BEAN ON A STRAW

A small pile of beans is placed on a table in front of each relay line. Each player is given a straw. At the word "go" the first player of each line runs forward, sucks a bean firmly onto the end of his straw, runs a designated distance and deposits the bean in a glass. Then the second player tries his luck. If a contestant drops his bean in transit, he automatically drops out and the next player in line starts. The line that gets the most beans transferred from the pile to the glass wins.

FEATHER RELAY

This can be played by a team of boys competing against a team of girls. Give the first in each line a feather. At a sign each one tries to keep his feather in the air by blowing on it while he crosses the room and returns. He then hands the feather to the next in line. The side finishing first wins the relay.

Variation: The feather can be laid on the floor and the contestant progresses on his hands and knees as he blows the feather to the goal line and back.

A feather can be given each group. The object is to keep the feather aloft. The group who first lets the feather fall to the floor loses. This gets to be a hilarious scramble.

WATER AND SPOON RACE

Contestants are divided into couples. One sits in a chair with head bent back, while the other contestant feeds him or her a half a glass of water teaspoon by teaspoon. Again a few may do this for the amusement of the whole group.

JAYWALKING

Players line up in two teams of equal numbers and the first one of each team is given a cane (a yardstick will do). The player rests his forehead on his hands on the cane handle, keeps his eyes on the floor, while he circles the cane six times. When he finishes the sixth round he walks to the opposite end of the room, touches a designated spot on the wall, then goes back to the starting point and yields the cane to the next contestant in line. The dizzy staggering of the contestants makes this a very funny game. Each contestant is sure he can do it without staggering, and usually fails. The line finishing first wins.

SACK BOP

Players stand in two lines. At the head of each line place a stack of No. 10 paper sacks; one for each player. At a given signal the first person in each line picks up a bag, runs to the end of his line, blowing it up as he runs and pops in on the back of the end player as he steps into line behind him. If the bag fails to burst, he blows it up and tries again. As soon as the explosion is heard the second person in line takes a turn with a sack. The side finishing first wins.

PULL AWAY

Draw a straight line about six feet long. Divide the group into two teams. Start the game with the first two players. Each player stands with both feet on the line, with heel and toe touching the line. Each contestant clasps the right hand of his opponent. Then by pulling each tries to make the other player lose his balance without losing his own. The one who stays on the line wins a point for his team. If both step off at the same time, they start over again. Continue this relay until each player has a turn. The team with the most points wins.

DRIVING RACE

Select two groups of three players each. In each group two of the players are horses. These two players make a seat of their hands, each player taking hold of his right wrist with his left hand, taking hold of the left wrist of the other player with his right hand. The horses are then blindfolded. The third player is then seated on this human chair. All three are turned around two or three times until the blindfolded horses lose all sense of direction. The signal to start is given and the two teams race across the room and back, the blindfolded horses being guided by the riders who direct them. The team getting across the room and back first are the winners.

FISHING

Line up the group into two lines. Give the first man of each team an ordinary pasteboard fan (a square of cardboard will do). In front of each team lay a small tissue-paper fish. Each man is supposed to fan his fish to the opposite end of the room and back—then pass the fan to the next man on his team. This relay is great fun as the fish flop in unpredictable directions. The first team to finish is the winner.

BALLOON RACE

Players of each team sit in a row on the floor, one directly back of the other, so that the two teams make two parallel rows. The first player in each row passes the balloon from the palm of his right hand to the palm of the right hand of the person behind him, who in turn follows suit—and so on down the line. The last player transfers the balloon to his left hand and passes it up the line again, this time by the left hand. At no time can the player touch the balloon with his free hand. If it falls off, the player behind picks it up with both hands and passes it on with one hand. The first team to return the balloon to the head of the line wins.

NUT TRUE OR FALSE

Players gather in the center of the room and are told the West end of the room is the False end and the East end the True. The leader reads a list of statements which he has prepared beforehand about nut subjects. For instance, the leader reads, "The peanut is a nut that grows above ground." The players race to the end of the room they think is correct. In this case the statement was False. Other nutty statements are:

The beechnut grows on the beach by the sea.

The hazelnut is a female nut.

The walnut is common in Minnesota.

The hickory nut grows on a tree famous for its wood.

The butternut comes from cows.

The chestnut is common around Christmas time.

The players guessing the most correct answers win.

CAR RELAY

For a lively game divide your group into teams with six players each, and have each team select the name of an automobile. Each player is given a part to play as follows:

1st player —Steering gear is broken—walk zigzag.
2nd player—Flat tire—limp.
3rd player—Water in gas—two steps forward—one back.
4th player—Can't go forward—walk backward.
5th player—Can't go at all.

6th player—Pushes fifth player by placing both hands on player's waist.

This is a walking relay in the usual line-relay formation. The team doing everything correctly and having the sixth player cross the finishing line first, wins the game.

RICHEST MAN

Players are divided into two lines. The first player in each row is given an empty quart milk bottle and a tablespoon. In front of each leader, placed on a table or stand before a mirror, put a dish of popcorn (unbuttered and unsalted). The object is to hold the bottle, top up, on the head and, while looking into the mirror, spoon as many kernels of popcorn into the bottle as possible in three tries.

Each player dumps his popcorn out of the bottle and counts the kernels while the next player tries his luck. The team finishing first frequently is not the winner. Often the slower players will have accumulated the most popcorn. Count each kernel worth $1000 and the total will tell which team is the richest.

FOOTPRINT RELAY

Ahead of time make paper footprints by drawing around the sole of a man's shoe on white wrapping paper. Cut them out and scotch tape them to the floor at various angles in two circles. Divide the group into two teams. At a signal the first player in each line starts. He must fit his foot exactly to each print in one circle. Each player completing his circle starts the next player in line on his team by touching him. The team that finishes first is winner.

RAINY-DAY RACE

The group is divided into two teams. An umbrella and a suitcase filled with old clothes are placed a few paces in front of each group. A skirt, or loose beach slacks, a flower hat and a pair of mittens make a hilarious costume. The object of the game is to have each contestant run to the suitcase, dress in the clothes, open the umbrella, race to a given goal, return with the suitcase and umbrella, close the umbrella, take off the clothes, repack them and pass the bag to the next player on the team. The excitement and hilarity in the dressing and packing reduces the onlookers to limpness from laughter.

HOOP ROLLING CONTEST

Two teams compete in rolling a hoop from a given point to a goal and back. This distance should be great enough to give each player a chance to demonstrate his hoop rolling skill. The team finishing first wins.

EGG RELAY RACE

Two hard-boiled eggs are used for this relay. The group is divided into two teams which form two lines, one player directly behind the other. Each player is given a teaspoon with instructions to hold the handle between his teeth. A hard-boiled egg is placed on the bowl of the spoon of each of the two leaders. At a signal the leaders, with their hands behind them, run to a goal across the lawn without dropping the eggs. If the player accomplishes it he grabs the spoon in his hand, runs back to the line and places the egg in the spoon of the player next in line.

If the player drops the egg in transit, he picks it up and places it back on the spoon before advancing farther. The team completing the race first is declared "Eggsperts."

EGG-CRACKING CONTEST

Each contestant holds an egg in his hand, small end up and challenges someone to crack his egg. The challenged player taps the egg of the challenger with his own egg. If the challenged cracks the egg of the challenger he wins the challenger's cracked egg. If his own is cracked, he turns it over to the challenger. This continues until only one uncracked egg remains and that player is declared, "The Great Uncracked." Needless to say, hard-boiled eggs are used for this game.

EGG TOSS

Each player faces a partner who stands about three feet away. The player tosses a raw egg to his partner. If his partner catches the egg without breaking it, each player takes one big step backwards. If the egg is not caught but smashes to the ground, that couple is eliminated. After each throw each partner moves backward one step. This game is most exciting if a number of teams are playing simultaneously.

CAT ON THE BACK FENCE

Divide the group into two teams. Stretch across the floor two parallel strips of white tape with ends pinned to the rug. (If the floor is bare use two parallel chalk marks.) This represents two back fences. The players become cats. The leaders of each team starting at the same time, back along the fence (tape or line) with both hands and feet on the fence. When they reach the other end of the fence they turn and travel back to where they began. As soon as the leaders are back the second one in line starts. The side finishing first wins the relay. This relay is exciting, requires skill and speed, and can be harmlessly played in a small space.

WASHINGTON CHERRIES

For a party on Washington's birthday, a cherry relay is a good game. Divide the players into two groups and assemble them in two lines. The first person in each line is given three large cherries. At a given signal each leader goes across the room and back balancing three cherries on the back of his left hand. If a cherry rolls off, the contestant has to pick it up unassisted and continue. Upon the leader's return, the second in line makes the journey, etc. The line finishing first wins the race.

BACKWARD RELAY

Players divide into two groups of equal number. Lay about two dozen rolled-up newspapers on the ground in two rows. The rows should be about eight feet apart and the newspapers should be laid at intervals of about two feet. Contestants must hop backwards over the newspapers to the goal and return. When the first player on each side returns, he touches off the next one. The side which finishes first wins the relay.

MATCH BOX RELAY

Divide the guests into two groups. Let the leader of each group fasten the cover of a penny match box on his own nose. Each must transfer the box cover from his nose to the nose of the next team mate without use of hands. If the cover is dropped, it may be picked up and put back on the nose of the last player to have it. The team that finishes passing the box first is the winner.

LIFE-SAVER RELAY

The group is divided into two lines. Each player is given a toothpick which he grips firmly between his front teeth. The first player of each team is given a Life Saver which he hangs on the toothpick in his mouth. At the word "Go" he transfers the Life Saver to the toothpick of the second in line without the use of hands. Of course, the team finishing first is declared the winner.

TOOTHPICK AND RAISIN RACE

Divide the players into two groups and line them up facing each other. Give each group a saucer of large raisins, enough to provide four raisins to each guest. Give each player a toothpick and have a team captain pass down the line with the saucer of raisins, and each team member must spear four raisins with the toothpick and eat them. The first group to finish wins.

DUNKING RELAY RACE

Teams are composed of two men each, who hold a doughnut apiece. A long table laden with cups of coffee is placed at the other end of the room. The first man of the relay team dashes to the other end of the room, dunks the doughnut in a cup of coffee, dashes back and feeds it to his teammate. The teammate must eat and swallow the doughnut, then dash out with his doughnut to repeat the other's performance. When the second doughnut is eaten and swallowed, the fastest team is proclaimed the winner.

HOOP JUMPING

Players are divided into two teams. The captain of each team holds a large hoop so that a player running from a given goal can jump through the hoop. The line jumping through its hoop first is declared the winner.

FRONT PAGE MOTHER GOOSE

Would you recognize some of the old Mother Goose rhymes if they were written in the style of a newspaper headline? For example, your morning and evening paper might use the following headline to explain how the marriage problem of Peter, Peter, Pumpkin Eater was solved: "Pumpkin Shell Solves Marriage Question."

For this game divide the guests into two teams. The hostess reads one of the headlines listed below to one team and gives the players half a minute in which to guess the rhyme. If none of the players can guess it, she reads the headline to the other team, then back again if there is still no answer. The team finally giving the correct rhyme may choose a player from the opposite team. After all the headlines have been called, the team with the largest number of players wins.

Headlines
1. Mother Spanks Daughter for Sitting in Cinders
2. Farmer's Wife Attacked by Blind Rodents
3. Girl Frightened by Spider
4. Men and Horses Fail to Revive Crash Victim
5. Married Couple Hearty Eaters
6. Wool Supply Assured, Inquiry Reveals
7. Unusual Pie Served Royalty
8. Dogs Herald Beggars Arrival
9. Pig Thief Punished
10. Violinists Give Command Performance for King
11. Pupil Queried About Tardiness
12. Woman Lacks Food—Dog Starves
13. People's Taste for Porridge Varies
14. Queen's Tarts Stolen; Thief Repents After Eating

Rhyme referred to in headlines
1. Little Polly Flinders Sat Among the Cinders
2. Three Blind Mice
3. Little Miss Muffet
4. Humpty Dumpty Sat On a Wall
5. Jack Sprat Could Eat No Fat, His Wife Could Eat No Lean
6. Bah, Bah, Black Sheep, Have You Any Wool?
7. Sing a Song of Sixpence
8. Hark! Hark; the Dogs Do Bark, the Beggars Are Coming to Town
9. Tom, Tom, the Piper's Son
10. Old King Cole
11. A Dillar, a Dollar, a Ten O'clock Scholar
12. Old Mother Hubbard
13. Pease Porridge Hot, Pease Porridge Cold
14. Queen of Hearts, She Made Some Tarts

5.

Challenges

Challenges should be a part of every program, whether it is a picnic, club meeting, small party, or large group. Frequently in challenges scores are kept to determine the winning team.

Challenges are of two types—physical and mental. Physical competition is very popular especially with boys of all ages. In smaller rooms, or when quiet games are needed, the mental tests come into their own. Boys and girls who are hesitant to display their lesser physical strength frequently excel in the mental competitions.

TESTS OF MENTAL SKILL

WRONG CAPITALS

One player names a State capital, placing it in the wrong state. The challenger must place it correctly before he takes his turn. For example, a player might say, "Des Moines is the capital of Utah." The challenger replies "Wrong! Des Moines is the capital of Iowa. St. Paul is the capital of Florida." The next in line must correctly locate St. Paul. One of the players may occasionally trip another by placing the capital in the right state. In this case he scores a point if his opponent erroneously corrects his statement.

MIXED DATES

This is a variation of the Wrong Capitals game. The first player mentions a well-known event but gives with it the date of some other event. The challenger must correct the date before he offers his own challenge. For example the first player might say, "Columbus discovered America in 1066." The challenger says, "Wrong! Columbus discovered America in 1492. The first satellite was sent around the earth in 1900." The second player will correct that date before he gives another event. Neither player may name an event for which he himself cannot give the correct date.

FARMER'S LOVE LETTER

This game will be enjoyed by couples working together. Give each couple a copy of "The Farmer's Love Letter." The blanks are to be filled in with fruits and vegetables. The couple finishing first wins the game.

The letter reads:

My darling sweet *(potato)*:

Do you *(carrot)* all for me? My heart *(beets)* for you, and my love is soft as a *(squash)*. I am for you as strong as an *(onion)*. You are a *(peach)* with your *(radish)* hair and *(turnip)* nose. You are the *(apple)* of my eye, so if we *(cantaloupe)*, then *(lettuce)* marry, for I know we will make a happy *(pear)*.

CITIES

The starter says "I'm going to Austin." The next in line must name a town beginning with the last letter of the city mentioned. In this case it could be "New York." That makes the next player search for a "K" like Keokuk or Kalamazoo or Kansas City.

PURCHASE

A player says, "I'm going to Chicago. What shall I buy?" The next to his right must respond with three things beginning with the first letter of the town the first player mentioned such as "Cows, cats and corn." The second player then says, "I'm going to St. Paul. What shall I buy?" And the next player names three things beginning with the letter "S." The purchases must be named before the next player can count to ten.

SNAP

Start the game off by pointing to a player, pronounce a word, then spell it, such as "Dog. D O G." Then immediately count to twelve—then say "Snap." Before you reach twelve the player to whom you have pointed must name three objects, the first beginning with D, the second with O, and the third with G. If he doesn't finish before you say "Snap," he is "IT" for the next time. Words of more than three letters can be used after a little practice in the game.

ADVERBS

Because there's a bit of actor in each of us, most everyone enjoys "Adverbs." The challenger thinks of an adverb and then proceeds to do what the players request him to do in the manner of the adverb he has thought of, such as "Wearily," "Hastily," "Ardently," etc. Then the group tries to guess what the adverb is.

MELODY MEMORIES

For this musical game decide upon the group of songs to be used—Old songs, popular songs, or perhaps hymns. The challenger then hums a line or two of a song, and the group must recognize the song, giving the title and the words of the line hummed.

PROVERBS

The challenger things of a proverb. The others ask any questions they please, but in his answer the challenger must use one word of the proverb. The questioner tries to discover the significant word in each answer until he can guess the proverb chosen. For instance, perhaps the proverb chosen is, "All that glitters is not gold." The questioner might ask, "Is your dress new?" and the answer might be, "Yes, but it doesn't glitter." The person who first guesses the proverb thinks up the next one.

JINGLE FUN

The challenger speaks one line to which the accepter must add a rhyming line before the challenger counts to ten. For example, the challenger might say, "Mary is a winner." The accepter might reply, "She's also a sinner." At first it is well to count to ten slowly and not to be too critical of the rhymes. As the players become skilled, correct rhyme and fairly good rhythm may be the standard.

ALIBI

A player asks the group some question like this: "Why can't you attend every meeting?" Give each person in the group three minutes to think of an excuse, using words beginning with his own initials. When the time is up, call for each excuse in turn. The sentence must begin with "Because I have to . . ." Mrs. J. M. Shaw would create a laugh by saying, "Because I have to Jump More Slowly." Charles W. Brown could say "Because I have to Cut Willie's Beard."

IMAGINARY SPY

A player thinks of an object in some special location; for instance, the latch on the school door. The others in the group try to find it by asking questions that may be answered by "Yes" or "No." The one who gets the right answer is "It" for the next game.

Variation: Have two people agree on the same object and take turns answering the questions.

DICTIONARY GAME

The person holding the dictionary chooses a simple, well-known subject such as shoes, silk, bread, etc., and reads the meaning of the word given in the dictionary. The reader uses "dashes" whenever the name of the subject is used, or whenever an obvious clue might give it away. The player who first guesses the subject chooses another subject and continues the game.

CONSONANT HUNT

What did the proud father say when he gave his son a tin horn? Have everyone write six "Os" in a line —for example, "oooooo." Tell the players that one consonant correctly sprinkled among the six "Os" gives the answer. The correct sentence will read the same forward or backward.

The answer—"Toot, Otto, Toot."

AN "M" QUIZ

It's a wise group that can answer this one without considerable discussion. According to the 1950 census there are twelve cities in the world over a half million population whose names all begin with "M." The United States has two such cities, but each of the others will be found in a different country of the world.

This game gets to be hilarious as the suggestions pour in, many of them incorrect.

The correct list: Melbourne, Australia; Madras, India; Moscow, Russia; Munich, Germany; Madrid, Spain; Montevideo, Uruguay; Manchester, England; Mexico City, Mexico; Montreal, Canada; Marseilles, France; Milwaukee, U. S. A.; Minneapolis, U. S. A.

Variation: If you wish to make the game competitive, divide the group into teams. The first group with a complete correct list is the winner.

EGO BUILDERS

Divide the entire group into seasons or months according to birth. Groups are then given three minutes each to describe why their particular month or season is the most interesting, or the best. A team of judges can decide the winner.

PARTNER COMPLIMENTS

This is a good teen-age or adult party. All draw numbers, those of the girls corresponding with those of the boys. The first man calls out his number, and compliments his unknown partner by telling her what he thinks is the loveliest thing about her. When he has finished, the lady with the number corresponding to his, steps out and is identified. This continues until everybody has a partner.

GEOGRAPHY

The leader holds up a card with a big "A" on it. The first one to call out the name of a city beginning with

"A" gets the "A" card. The leader next displays a "B" and the promptest one in naming a town beginning with "B" gets the "B" card. This continues until all twenty-six letters of the alphabet are distributed. The one who collects the largest number of letters becomes leader for the next game.

THE PRINCE OF PARIS

The leader says, "The Prince of Paris went to London to buy a feathered fan," and makes a fan-like motion with his right hand. Each player repeats after him. Next time the leader adds, "A feathered fan and a pair of scissors," again with the appropriate motion. The next addition is a hobby horse and the final one a coo-coo clock with the added action being that each person says "coo-coo, coo-coo." A fitting ending.

DEBATE

For this game choose four of the most articulate in the group. Announce the subject—"Resolved, that it is better to be fat than slim." Let the two slimmest argue the affirmative, and the two fattest the negative. Constructive speeches last three minutes and rebuttal two minutes. At the close of arguments let three judges choose the winning team. This is an hilarious game as each debater warms up to his subject.

THE MOON IS ROUND

The players sit in a circle. The leader stoops and with his left hand outlines a face on the floor, saying,

"The moon is round, it has two eyes, a nose, and a mouth." The others must stoop and do the same. If they do not use their left hands, they have failed to do it properly because their imitation of the leader was not exact. Clearing the throat before starting, putting one hand on the hip, standing with a knee bent, and outlining one's own face with the left hand are variations the leader may use.

GHOSTS

The object of the game of "Ghosts" is to add a letter to the word that is being spelled but to avoid finishing the word. Anyone who finishes a word becomes a third of a ghost and when he is three-thirds be must drop out. The first player names any letter of the alphabet. The second adds another letter that can be used in spelling some word but that will not finish the word. Thus, if the first player said "B" and the second—thinking of "Best"—adds "E," he becomes a third of a ghost because "Be" is a word in itself. When a word is finished the next player starts another. At any time a player may challenge another concerning the word he is spelling. If the player who is challenged is not spelling a word that he has actually in mind, he becomes a third of a ghost. If he can cite a word, the player who challenged him becomes a third of a ghost.

MY FATHER'S A MERCHANT

In this game the players try to guess what it is that makes the statements true or false. The leader turns to his neighbor and says, "My father's a merchant." The neighbor asks, "What does he sell?" The leader may reply, "Cotton goods." He must be sure to touch something cotton as he speaks. The person addressed then repeats these statements to his next neighbor. If he has noticed the leader's procedure, he will also touch whatever he says his father sells. If he has failed to observe it—and probably he will—the leader may laughingly say, "Oh, no, he doesn't," or "That isn't true."

As the players in turn make their statements, the leader remarks whether they are right or not until the group has guessed the trick.

TWO LITTLE BLACKBIRDS

The leader fastens a tiny piece of gummed paper on the nail of each of his middle fingers. He extends these fingers on his knee and recites the following, accompanying the words with the gestures indicated:

Two little blackbirds sitting on a hill,

One named Jack (lift right finger)

One named Jill (lift left finger)

Fly away, Jack (quickly throw right hand to shoulder, bringing it down with the index instead of middle finger extended)

Fly away, Jill (do the same with left hand)

Come back, Jack (repeat with right hand but extend middle instead of index finger)

Come back, Jill (do same with left hand).

MR. GOONY

The leader says, "Mr. Goony is a loony, but he's not crazy. He likes walls and doors, but not ceilings. He likes tennis and volleyball, but not badminton." The object of the game is for each guest to catch on why Mr. Goony is loony but not crazy. Often players will think it is the alphabetical placement of letters or anything but the simple fact that Mr. Goony likes only those things which are spelled with double letters like loony, walls and doors, but not things which contain only single letters, like crazy. There's no limit on this game. It should be continued only as long as the solution is still a mystery to some and the whole group is interested.

GOING TO INDIA

The leader whom we shall call Carl says, "I'm going to India next week." Then he says that he is going to take something with him which begins with the first letter of his first name. For example, Carl might say, "I'm going to take some candy because maybe in India I won't be able to get any sweets."

Then turning to someone else he says, "What would you like to take to India?" That person in turn is supposed to take something which starts with the first letter of his own first name. If his answer is wrong the traveler says, "Oh, I'm sorry. You can't come. Besides candy, I'm going to take a case of corn. I would miss corn for dinner if I couldn't get any in India." Then turning to another person, "What would you like to take to India?" And so on until he finds someone who catches on and can also go to India. This continues with those who have guessed always adding another thing they are going to take till the entire group is in the know.

MUSICAL SPELLDOWN

Divide the party into two groups who stand facing each other. The leader plays or sings snatches of tunes. If the first player at the head of the line cannot name the tune being played or hummed, he sits down. Then the player at the head of the opposite line takes his chance and so on down the two lines. The last one to stand is the winner.

TWENTY QUESTIONS

The player who is designated as "It" thinks of some specific object and states whether it is animal, vegetable, or mineral. The object may be real or fictional and may be located anywhere in the world. The other players then have twenty questions in which to determine what the object is. Each question must be answered by "yes," "no," or "partly." The players take turns in asking questions. The player who is "It" keeps track of the number of questions that have been asked, and the one guessing the object correctly is "It" for the next round of the game. If no one guesses the answer after twenty questions have been asked, "It" is the winner and may select another object to be guessed.

MEMORY SELECTIONS

The challenger gives a quotation from some specified field such as the Bible, poetry, or some famous speech. Or if he wishes, he can announce before beginning that he will use quotations from any source. When the challenger has recited his chosen quotation the players, one at a time, take turns in guessing the sources from which the quotation was taken. The one who guesses the correct source then takes his turn as challenger and gives a quotation to be identified. If no one can guess the quotation, the challenger names his source, and gives another quotation.

Variation: For an easier form of this game, the challenger may quote a line of poetry. Other players in turn try to add the next line. For instance, the challenger says, "Early to bed and early to rise." A guesser can reply, "Makes a man healthy, wealthy, and wise."

BROADCASTING

This stunt gives young hopefuls a chance to use some lovely big words, copying some of the radio comedians. Each player takes his turn in making the longest sentence he can, beginning each important word with the beginning letter of his last name. For instance, Smith might say: "So long, sister, see you soon in San Francisco, selling silly symphonies to sarcastic sobsters." It is well to give players from three to five minutes to think up their lingo, then let each take his turn to spout. A prize can go to the player with the most words in his sentence or the most sense in his speech.

RUMOR CLINIC

For a large crowd this game works best if you can throw a picture on a sheet or screen large enough for the entire crowd to see. Before the picture is shown ask four people to leave the room. Give the audience five minutes to study the picture. Then ask one of the audience to call in one person from the back room. The two stand facing the audience with their backs to the picture. The one who has seen the picture describes what he saw in the picture to player No. 2. Then player No. 1 takes his seat. Player No. 2, still without looking at the picture, calls in player No. 3 and tells him what player No. 1 saw in the picture. Player No. 3 repeats the story to player No. 4. This is a hilarious game because all the time the audience can see the picture and see the mistakes being repeated and made by the contestants. It is a good game to teach the fallacy of believing in rumor.

AIR, WATER, AND FIRE

The one who is "It" points to one of the players and calls out one of the three words, "Air," "Water" or "Fire" and then quickly counts to ten. The player designated must name an animal living in the element called; unless the word "Fire" is called, then he makes no answer. For instance, in answer to "Air" a player can say "Blue jay" or "Dog." If he fails to answer correctly before ten is counted, or if he mentions an animal another player has already mentioned, he then becomes "It."

MOTION SPELLING

Everyone is seated in a circle. The leader chooses two letters, for instance "E" and "T," and announces that these letters must not be said aloud, but that "E" is to be indicated by raising the right hand and "T" by raising the left. For example, the word "BET" would be spelled like this: "B" pronounced, right hand raised for "E," left hand raised for "T." In giving out words the leader should choose as many as he can think of containing the letters "E" and "T" (butter, better, eat, meat, etc.). As a player misses a motion or pronounces a silent letter, he drops out. The player staying in the longest wins.

For an older group more difficult words can be used and more difficult rules. For instance, for "E" raise the right hand, "T" left hand, "I" touch the eye, "U" point to the leader, "R" hum or whistle and "S" nod the head.

ADD-A-LETTER PUZZLE

This word puzzle starts with one letter at the top and ends with a six letter word at the bottom. Add one letter to each word to form the next word. Work the puzzle with these clues.

1. ☐

2. ☐ ☐

3. ☐ ☐ ☐

4. ☐ ☐ ☐ ☐

5. ☐ ☐ ☐ ☐ ☐

6. ☐ ☐ ☐ ☐ ☐ ☐

1. Fourth letter in the alphabet
2. Short for advertisement
3. Owned
4. Opposite of soft
5. Strong
6. Scarcely

Here's the solution:

1. D
2. A D
3. H A D
4. H A R D
5. H A R D Y
6. H A R D L Y

Here are some additional ADD-A-LETTER puzzles that can be worked out with a similar chart.

		Answers
1.	First letter of the alphabet	A
2.	Because	AS
3.	Short for gasoline	GAS
4.	Openings	GAPS
5.	Yawns	GAPES
6.	Kind of fruit	GRAPES

		Answers
1.	Eighth letter of the alphabet	H
2.	A man or boy	HE
3.	Opposite of "him"	HER
4.	Listen to	HEAR
5.	Design used for Valentines	HEART
6.	Cordial	HEARTY

		Answers
1.	Second letter of the alphabet	B
2.	Exist	BE
3.	Piece of furniture	BED
4.	Raised	BRED
5.	Uncovered	BARED
6.	Divided by bars	BARRED

NUMBER WIZARDRY

Ask someone to write a number of four figures and just under it another number of four figures. Then you write a number of four figures just under in the same column. Your friend then writes another number of four figures in the same column and you write a fifth number of four figures.

At any time your friend writes down the first number you will be able to announce the total of the column of five figures. When your friend finds by adding the column that your total is correct he will be much impressed with your wizardry.

Here's how it is done.

Suppose your friend writes	1187
and	5624
You write	4375
He writes	4088
You write	5911
Total	21,185

Subtract two from the last figure of the first number in the column and put the figure two just before that number. In the case cited above two from seven equals five. By placing the figure two before the number you have 21, 185. That will be the total of the column of figures if you follow a certain rule when you write in your figures. Your friend may write any number of four digits he wishes, but when it is your turn to write, each figure you put down must, added to the number above it, equal nine.

For example in this case your friend put down 5624.

For your turn you wrote	4375
Each digit adds a 9	9999

Follow this same rule when you write the fifth row of figures in the column. Your fifth figure added to his fourth must total nine for each digit.

Travel Fun

Going on a family auto trip soon? When the telephone poles seem to be zooming by in an endless procession, and the scenery looks all the same, beat old man Monotony with a game. Try some of these. They're fun.

COLOR CONTEST

With all the fancy colored cars on the road, a color contest is exciting. Divide the carload into two teams. One team watches for the cars painted with the primary colors—Red, Yellow, or Blue. The other team looks for cars painted the secondary colors, Orange, Green, and Purple. The object of the game is to see two cars of each color. A two-colored-car painted with both a primary and a secondary color can be counted by each team. The team first completing its list wins.

LICENSE PLATE DOUBLES

Each passenger takes a number such as 1, 2, 3, 4, and 5. Then each one watches the license numbers of approaching cars. If a license plate has two numbers alike, or a pair of numbers, such as 34556, player No. 1 gets a total of the pair as his score. In this case he adds 5 plus 5 or a total of 10 to his score. The total of the next pair of numbers seen should be credited to player No. 2, and so on until each player has had a turn for a score. Then it is No. 1's turn again. If the license on a passing car has no doubles, the player whose turn it is adds nothing to his score. If a license number has more than two like digits, the lucky player adds the sum of all like digits to his score. For instance, if the license is 54556—that player could add 15 to his score. The first player to accumulate a score of 100 is winner.

DISTANCE GAME

If you're traveling in the mountains, or in hilly country, or even on a long stretch of level road where distances are deceiving, it's fun to play "How Far." Look ahead to a hill, lake, or next town. At a signal everyone guesses "How Far" it is. Then watch the speedometer to see whose guess is right. Maybe you'll have a guessing expert in your car.

ANIMAL HUNT

When whizzing through the country it's fun to watch for livestock. Divide into two teams of watchers —one for each side of the road. The team first seeing all ten of the following list wins: Red cow, White horse, Brown chicken, Black lamb, Black and white pig, Spotted pig, White turkey, Bronze turkey, Black bull, White duck.

STATE GAME

If you are driving through the country on a long trip, it's fun to spot cars from as many different states as possible. Try keeping a list to see which one can get a complete list of the forty-nine states first. For instance, if Dad spots a car from Maine—that counts for Dad only. Credit can be given only to the one who spots the license first. The others will have to find other Maine cars for their own lists.

ONE HUNDRED

For this game number yourselves 1, 2, 3, and 4. On the next approaching car, note the first and last digits of the license plate. Add them together and credit the total to player No. 1. Total from the two corresponding digits of the second car will be credited to player No. 2. The player whose total first reaches 100 wins.

PAIRS

A variation of the above game is to count only the digits which appear in pairs. For instance, if a car has a number which reads 34556, add the two 5s and credit the player with a total of ten. Pass up all cars without a double in the license number. The first player whose total reaches 100 wins.

TEN PAIRS

Another license plate game that is fun is for each player to choose a different digit as his number. One might choose 5 as his number. He scans each license plate for a pair of 5s. Three 5s would count as two pairs, and four 5s as four pairs. All players score on any license number that bears a pair of their chosen digits. For example, a passing car might bear the license No. 64,564. The player who has chosen 6 would count a pair as could the player who chose 4. The first player who finds ten pairs wins.

U AUTO KNOW

Here is a guessing contest that will make your wits tingle. Each phrase can be answered with the name of an automobile.

Questions	Answers
A crossing	Ford
A rock in New England	Plymouth
A river in New York State	Hudson
A president of the U. S.	Lincoln
A wild animal	Jaguar
Two initials	M. G.
A chemical liquid	Mercury
The capital of Texas	Austin
Part of the capital of Tennessee	Nash
A musician's name (misspelled)	Chrysler
A Spanish explorer	De Soto

After this game has been played as a Riddle, it can become a Highway Contest. The first one to spot on the highway the make of car answering each question would be the winner.

GOAT CONTEST

Who can see the most goats? One player or team can watch one side of the road while the other team watches the other side. The object of the game is to spot, within an agreed time— say thirty or sixty minutes—the greatest number of goats. Each side keeps its own score.

If one team sees a church on its side of the road, all scores are wiped out and the team starts counting all over again.

Variation: Goats need not be the only animal sought. If you wish any animal, such as horses, pigs, mules, or sheep may be substituted.

WHEE

Here's a game to sharpen the wits. The players watch the countryside for objects to "Whee." The scoring goes like this: white horse, 1 point; white mule, 5 points; white goat 10 points; and white bearded man, 25 points. The first player to see one of these objects shouts, "Whee, mule." If it proves to be a mule, he scores 5 points; if not, he loses 5 points. Set a definite score or a period of time to end the game.

ALPHABET

This game can be played by two players with each taking one side of the road. The object of the game is to complete the alphabet by picking in sequence the letters from sign board or direction signs along the highway. Sometimes when the letter N is reached by one player, sides of the road are swapped. The player arriving at Z first wins.

6.

Challenges: Tests of Physical Skill

BOTTLE WRESTLE

This game is especially good for active boys. Divide your group into pairs, matching the boys as to size and age. Place a milk bottle on the floor. The two boys stand facing each other with hands on the other's shoulders. The object of the game is to see which boy can pull or push his partner until he forces him to bump over the bottle. The one who bumps over the bottle is of course the loser.

This game can be played tournament style. Several twosomes can be playing at a time. All the winners will then play each other until there is only one winner left.

TOE TILT

Two players sit on the floor facing each other with their knees bent, their feet flat on the floor, and their arms clasped around their legs. Under the knees and over the arms of each is thrust a wand or broomstick. At a signal each player tries to lift with his toes the feet of his opponent. The one who succeeds, thus compelling his opponent to lose his balance and roll over on his back, wins the contest.

BROOMSTICK BALANCE

A bridge is made by laying a broomstick on the seats of two chairs a slight distance apart. With the aid of a cane the contestant seats himself on the broomstick and crosses his legs. When he is nicely balanced he tries to remove with his cane two handkerchiefs that have been hung on the back of the chair behind him. Three falls are allowed before he is declared a loser.

STICK PULL

Two players sit on the ground, each having the soles of his feet pressed against those of his opponent. They grasp a stick and hold it crosswise above their toes. At a signal each tries to pull the other to a standing position. The player who is pulled up, or over, or who releases the stick, is the loser.

STICK WRESTLE

Two players grasp a stick with both hands. At a signal each tries to get the stick away from his opponent by any twisting or pulling method. The contest is not ended until one player has gained complete possession of the stick.

TWIST STICK

Two players face each other, extend their arms overhead, and grasp a stick. At a signal they step backward and pull the stick down between them, each trying to retain his own grip and make the stick slip in his opponent's hands. The one who loses control of the stick loses the contest.

JUG KNOT

Each contestant sits on a large jug turned sideways. He must extend his legs, hold the knees straight, and put the heel of one foot on the upturned toes of the other. In this position he must tie a knot in a handkerchief. If he does not keep his knees straight until the knot is finished, he loses the contest.

BAG BOXING

Have on hand a number of paper bags large enough to fit loosely over the head. Place a bag on the head of each of two contestants extending down to his ears. At a given signal they box with open hands, or rolled newspapers, trying to knock the other fellow's hat off. They are not permitted to touch their own hats. This, too, can be played tournament style. A number of boxing contests can be played simultaneously. The winners can all play each other until only one winner remains.

ARE YOU THERE, CHARLIE?

Two blindfolded players lie stretched out on the floor facing each other and join their left hands. Each holds a rolled newspaper in his right hand. One of them says, "Are you there, Charlie?" The other answers, "Yeaaah." Whereupon No. 1 swings his swatter in the direction from which the answer came, while No. 2 ducks his head. Then No. 2 asks the question. Give each contestant ten tries, score each hit a point. For added fun, after the game has progressed awhile, the leader may slip the blindfold from one of the players and allow the stunt to go on.

NEEDLE THREADER

This game is usually played by girls but might be fun for boys too. Contestant sits on round milk bottle laid lengthwise on the floor. She is given a needle and thread. With legs straight out so that no part of the body is touching the floor, she attempts to thread the needle. If a group of girls are trying this stunt simultaneously, the first to succeed is adjudged agile enough to be the first to catch a husband.

CHICKEN FIGHT

Two players stand in a circle drawn about eight feet in diameter. They stoop and grasp their own ankles. At a signal each tries to push the other from the circle or out of balance. A player loses when he leaves the circle, releases either hand, or touches the ground with any part of his body except his feet.

HAND PUSH

Two contestants stand facing each other with their toes touching. They have their palms also touching on a level with their chests. In this position each pushes the other's hands until one is forced to step back. The player who forces his opponent backward is the winner.

CHINESE GET-UP

Group pairs off. Two sit on floor, back to back, with locked arms. At a signal they try to rise. This, too, lends itself to tournament play. The winners play each other until only one winner remains.

DOUBLE HANDCUFFS

Be ready with two strings forty inches long. Tie each end of one of the strings around the boy's wrists. The second string is passed between the boy's string and his body and the ends of it tied to each of the girl's wrists, thus linking the two together. The object is for the couple to free themselves without breaking or untying the strings. It's loads of fun to watch a couple struggle to get free, stepping through the loop, putting it over their heads, and the like.

Sooner or later some bright youngster will discover the trick, and the gang will be much disconcerted with its simplicity. The handcuffed boy picks up his string, puts it under the string on the inside of the girl's wrist, over her hand, down the back of her hand and under the string. Presto, the couple is free, although the strings are unbroken and still fastened to the wrists.

ROOSTER FIGHT

Two players face each other in a circle drawn about six feet in diameter. Each puts his right hand behind his back, clasps his left foot with it, and then grips his right arm with his left hand behind his back. In this position they hop at each other when a signal is given. Each tries to force the other out of the circle or out of position. As soon as a player lets go of a foot or arm or leaves the circle, he loses the game.

BOWLEGGED DUTCHMAN

All youngsters are familiar with jumping rope, either one alone or with two swinging the rope. For extra fun, add a rhyme such as "Bow-legged Dutch-man."

A bow-legged Dutchman (Jump with bow legs)

Walking down the street

A bow-legged Dutchman

Won't you have a seat (Squat between jumps)

A bow-legged Dutchman

Take a bite of bun (Imitate taking a bite)

A bow-legged Dutchman

You'd better run! (Run out of line and new jumper jumps in.)

BEE AND FLOWER

All players with the exception of one line up in a single file, each one holding on to the waist of the person in front. The remaining player becomes a sunflower. The object of the game is for the entire line of bees to ensnare the "flower." To catch the flower, the head and tail of the line must surround the flower and enclose him or her in the circle. The game is so much fun it can be repeated many times with a different flower each time.

STATUE

In this old favorite, played by many generations of children, one child is the "twirler." The twirler grabs the right hand of each player and swings him around three times. The players hold the position in which they land. The twirler looks them over and picks the most interesting one to be the next twirler.

VIRGINIA REEL

This is an old folk game, well enjoyed by young people of every generation. The players stand well apart in lines or sets of about six couples facing each other. The boys' line is at the left of the girls when they turn to march. All the couples go through the figures at the same time. While the music is being played or sung the leader should call the figures as follows:

Foreward and Bow:	Each player advances three steps, bows to his partner and returns to his place.
Right hand swing:	Partners advance, join their right hands, and turn each other.
Left hand swing:	Partners join their left hands and turn.
Both hands swing:	Partners join both hands and turn.
Do Si Do Right:	Partners fold arms and walk around each other, passing on the right and walking backward to place.
Do Si Do Left:	Partners fold arms and walk around, passing on the left and walking backward to place.

Arm Right:	Partners hook their right arms and swing around.
Arm Left:	Partners hook their left arms and swing around.
Head Couples Lead Your Lines Away:	The girl in the first couple turns to the right and the boy to the left, and the others follow. They march down outside their respective lines, clapping hands in time to the music. When the first couple meets at the foot of the lines, they join hands and form a bridge. As the following couples meet they march under the bridge to their places, the second couple thus becoming the first. The game is continued until each couple has acted as first couple.

TUB OF CORKS

Put to float a large number of small corks in a tub of water. It is well to use a tub or at least a large dish-pan so that the corks cannot be easily pushed against the bottom. Give a contestant a pin and tell him to spear as many corks as he can in three minutes. The cork must not be touched by hand, neither may it touch the sides of the pan while being harpooned. If your tub is ample, two players can be spearing at the same time. But don't pass out pins to the players until they are ready for their turn at the tub, or some practical joker will be sure to harpoon a guest or two.

PRISONER

Players form a line across one end of the yard or room. The one who is It stands about thirty feet away, with his back turned, and spells "P-R-I-S-O-N-E-R" and then says "CAUGHT." Meanwhile the players run toward him, stopping just before he gets to the end. As one who is It says "Caught," he turns around quickly and if he catches anyone moving, that player must go back to the starting line. First player to run up and tag the player wins five points and then he is It.

HORSESHOE

For an indoor game use a child's game of horseshoe with the stakes on metal standards and hard rubber horseshoes. These rubber shoes are really much harder to throw than the kind Old Dobbin wore. Nevertheless, the same rules apply—game is fifty points. Ringing the stake counts three points. If the player makes a ringer with both shoes he is credited with six points. Points are awarded also for position. The nearest one to the stake scores one point. If both nearest belong to the same player he gets two points. A combination of one ringer and one shoe nearest the stake counts four points. Only one player scores in a turn. If both players make ringers each cancels the other. If the horseshoes of opponents are equidistant from the stake, no points are awarded either of the players.

DUCK ON ROCK

"Duck on Rock" is loads of fun to play out in the open. Each player must have a bean bag, which is called his duck. A large rock or a stump is chosen as the duck rock and twenty-five feet from it a line is drawn. Each player throws his duck from this line. The one whose duck falls nearest the rock becomes the first guard. He lays his duck on the rock and stands by it.

The other players then stand behind the line and take turns in throwing their ducks at the duck on the rock, trying to knock it off. After each throw a player must recover his own duck and run home (back of the line). If he is tagged by the guard while trying to do this, he must change places with the guard. The guard may tag him whenever he is in front of the line, unless he stands with his foot on his own duck where it fell. He may stand thus as long as he wishes, awaiting a chance to run home; but the moment he lifts his duck from the ground or takes his foot from it, he may be tagged. He is not allowed to lay his duck on the ground again after he has once lifted it to run.

The guard must not tag any player unless his own duck is on the rock. If it has been knocked off, he must pick it up and replace it before he may chase anyone. This replacing gives the thrower who knocked it off some time to recover his own duck and run home. As long as the guard's duck stays on the rock, several throwers may have to wait before they can try to recover their ducks.

A player tagged by the guard must put his own duck on the rock and become the guard. The one who is no longer the guard must get his duck from the rock and run for the line as quickly as possible, because he can now be tagged as soon as the new duck is on the rock.

If a duck falls very near the rock without knocking the guard's duck off, the guard may challenge its thrower by calling "Span!" This gives him time to measure with his hand the distance between the rock and that duck. If the distance is shown to be less than a span (the distance from the end of the thumb to the end of the little finger), the thrower must change places with the guard as if he had been tagged.

"Duck on Rock" also can be played in an indoor recreation room because it does not entail running great distances and even the most rotund can compete. Also strategy enters in to such an extent that frequently strategy can often offset greater agility.

MOCK OLYMPICS

A good game with huge crowds—can be played with twenty-five, fifty, or one hundred. Break the crowd down into smaller groups. Each group selects a country. Younger crowds like to make up a yell for their country. If time is available beforehand, each group can dress in the costume of its country. Different colored crepe paper can be given each group from which to make streamers or sashes.

One from each group participates in a sports event, such as:

1. Javelin Throw—throw straws for distance.
2. Discus Throw—throw paper plates for distance.
3. One mile race—foot race, heel to toe.
4. Fifty-yard dash—run a stated distance, eat a peach turned upside down in a saucer without using the hands. The first one to stand up after eating the peach wins.
5. Shot-put—eat crackers, blow up a balloon; first one to pop the balloon wins.
6. One hundred-yard dash—run a stated distance, thread a needle at end of run.

7. Hurdles—sprinkle peanuts along a course; contestant has to shell and eat peanuts on way to goal.

8. Tug-O-War—Marshmallow with string threaded through center—contestant on each end of string—first one to chew string to marshmallow and eat the marshmallow wins.

9. Hammer Throw—blow up paper bags and tie string around the top — contestant whirls paper bag around head by the string and then throws. The farthest one wins.

10. Medley Relay—(Underwater relay)

   1—Duck Walk

   2—Crab Walk

   3—Contestant has bathing cap on head, cardboard flipper on feet, olympic torch in hand. The object is to put on all these things and then race to the goal.

11. Accuracy Toss—egg toss—each group against another group (even in numbers)—face each other in one long line—first two people in each group toss egg between them—continues down line to farthest two people away from each other—last group keeping the egg whole wins.

12. Cheer Judging — judging done by leader or group of three judges chosen by the group. Each group gives one cheer.

Hints for Mock Olympics

1—Have each group make up songs and cheers for their country and come to the olympics dressed in costumes of that country. The costumes need not be too elaborate or authentic. May be made of crepe paper, etc., whatever the group wants to buy.

2—Have a parade going from school to the field—olympics held on the football field.

3—Could have a player dressed in an outlandish costume run across the field holding the olympic torch and present the torch to the MC to start the program. Torch can be made of tin foil and red paper.

4—Have players pick a country as soon as possible so they will have time to plan.

5—Have a committee of six or more to help set up and judge the events.

6—Award first, second and third place on certain events, such as javelin throw, discus throw, one hundred yard dash, hammer throw, shot put, etc.

CONTRARIES

Choose a leader who picks his victim. The victim is to do the opposite of what the leader does. Both are provided with chairs and hats. When the leader stands the victim sits. When the leader puts on his hat the victim takes his off. They should act simultaneously. It is almost impossible to do the opposite while watching the leader, much to the enjoyment of the watching crowd. After a bit have the victim be the leader and choose someone who has laughed long and hard to be the victim.

BROOMSTICK RACE

Lay a broomstick on the floor. Place your elbow next to the broom handle and measure the distance to your finger tips. Put an apple on that spot. Then kneel on the broomstick, keeping both hands on the stick, and pick up the apple with your teeth. The chances are you'll land on your nose the first try.

BACK TO BACK LIFT (Boys only)

Two contestants stand back to back with elbows linked. At a signal each, by pulling and bending forward, attempts to lift the other off the ground. The one lifted off the ground loses the bout. Three bouts are a match.

BACK TO BACK PUSH (Boys only)

Two players of about equal size stand back to back with both arms linked at the elbows. Establish a line ten feet in front of each contestant. At a signal, each contestant attempts to drag the opponent over his base line. Lifting and carrying of the opponent are permitted. The contestants must keep their original positions with arms linked. The contestant carried across his opponent's base line loses. Best two out of three bouts wins the match.

7.

Paper and Pencil Games

Sharpen the pencils and pass out the paper to the play-ers with keen wits. There's many a paper and pencil game worth playing that will let the players catch their breath after more strenuous games.

SOLVING THE CRIME

Seat the players in a circle and give each one a pencil and a sheet of paper. Explain that a murder has been committed and they are all asked to help solve the mystery. Then ask them to write as near the top of the paper as possible, "The body of" and the name of one of the guests. Then fold over the paper just enough to cover the writing and pass to the next player on the left. Continue in this way, asking them to write the fol-lowing, one phrase at a time, and after writing each phrase, folding over and passing the paper:

was found at (name a place)

(name another player) is suspected of the crime
because (give a reason)
The victim was killed by (give a method)
The motive was ....
The verdict is ....
The sentence is ....

When all have completed writing the phrases, the
papers are passed again. Each one opens up the paper
passed to him and reads it aloud, much to the merriment of the crowd.

NAME HER

This is a questionnaire that can be answered by
girls' names.   *Answers*

1. What an army would do if it found a river.	Bridget
2. An admirable quality in a young woman.	Charity
3. The most prominent of Easter flowers.	Lily
4. The time for violets.	May
5. A gem.	Opal
6. What baby is to papa.	Delight
7. The flower of June.	Rose
8. What a scissors-grinder and a locomotive have in common.	Bell
9. A virtue.	Faith
10. An article.	Ann
11. First step in music.	Dora
12. The night before.	Eve
13. A little valley.	Dale

MIRROR DRAWING

The player slants a mirror so he can look into it
and see the surface of the paper placed before it. He

watches the reflection and not the paper. The leader asks him to draw a single diagram consisting of straight down, cross and diagonal lines. The cross and up and down lines are fairly easy to draw; but on the diagonal lines, the hand seems to have lost all sense of direction. Next experiment with curves, circles, and writing a name.

WORD CHART

Each player is given a paper and pencil. A word of five or six letters is chosen such as "people." Each player makes himself a chart by printing the letters of this word in a column down the left side of a sheet of paper, then on the right side in reverse order.

For example, if the word "people" is used, the chart will look like this:

P	E
E	L
O	P
P	O
L	E
E	P

The object of this game is to fill the space in the lines between these letters. The first line requires a word that starts with "P" and ends with "E" such as "PADDLE" or "PEE WEE." The second line requires a word beginning with "E" and ending with "L," and so on.

The players should use the longest words they can think of, because one point is scored for every letter added by the player.

UNITED STATES

Provide each player with a card and pencil and announce that ten minutes will be allowed for the players to list as many states in the United States as they can. Even fairly young children are familiar with most of the states in the Union and will enjoy the contest. If the group is a little older, ask them to list the capitals of each state.

FLOWERS

This is an ideal game for garden club members or other flower lovers. Give each player a card on which to write his or her initials. Ask the players to exchange cards. Then direct each one to write the name of a flower beginning with the last initial, and two descriptive words beginning with the first two initials. For instance, B. F. V. might be filled in to be Big Fat Violet. S. B. N. might be interpreted to be Sun Burned Nasturtium.

The cards are then returned to the original holder. Each player then reads the flowery interpretation of his or her own initials.

NUT BANK

Beforehand, put as many small objects as you can in an empty walnut shell. Amazingly you can crowd in about twenty objects, such as a rubber band, a bobby pin, a pin, eraser from a pencil, a bit of string, scrap of tissue paper, tiny thimble, small earring, a navy bean, piece of rice, kernel of corn, a human hair, paper clip, etc. Stick the shell together with cellulose tape.

Give each player a pencil and paper and ask him to list the things that he thinks might be hidden in the walnut shell. Amaze the player by telling him there are twenty, twenty-one or whatever number of objects there are in the nut shell.

At the close of ten minutes, open the shell. Each player checks his list with the actual contents in the shell. A prize goes to the one with the most nearly correct list.

CAT WORDS

Players are provided with papers and pencils. The leader reads the following questions. Each answer begins with the word or syllable "Cat."

	Answers
1. What cat makes trouble?	Catastrophe
2. What cat is a sauce?	Catsup
3. What cat is a plant that grows in marshes?	Cat-tail
4. What cat has horns?	Cattle
5. What cat is a person used as a tool?	Cat's-paw
6. What cat lived in Rome long ago?	Cato
7. What cat is learned in church?	Catechism
8. What cat is sent out by mail order houses?	Catalogue
9. What cat is a waterfall?	Cataract
10. What cat is wild?	Catamount
11. What cat is a plant of the mint family?	Catnip
12. What cat is a disease?	Catarrh
13. What cat is an ancient burying place?	Catacomb
14. What cat is an instrument of torture?	Cat-o-nine-tails

15. What cat is a bird?	Catbird
16. What cat is a church?	Catholic
17. What cat is a fish?	Catfish
18. What cat prepares food?	Caterer
19. What cat is a flower?	Catkin

The one with the most correct answers is the winner.

WORD BUILDING

Give each player a paper and pencil. Then read five or six one-syllable words such as: he, ten, son, dun, bad, can. The object of the game is for each player to make as long a word as he can around each of the six words on the list. For instance, one player, using the word "dun," might think of dune, another of dungeon, and still a third of redundant. At the close of a ten minute playing time, the player with the longest words wins the prize.

DARK DOG

Each player is given a four-by-six blank card and a pencil. The players are warned to take a good look at the card because they are going to be blindfolded. When all are blindfolded they are asked to draw a dog on their card. After this they are told to put a collar on the dog. Then to draw a bone in front of him. And then to draw a license tag hanging from his collar. The blindfolds are then removed and the astounding pictures exhibited.

GUESS IT

Divide the group into teams of four and seat them around card tables. One of each team leaves the room.

The leader assigns to these players some subject. Each player returns to his table and without confiding his subject to his team-mates, draws the subject assigned him. It may be a picture of Betsy Ross at work on the first flag or any other picture. If the would-be artists have no artistic ability so much the funnier. The object of the game is for the players at each table to guess just what their team-mate is drawing. The table guessing the subject first is the winner.

SQUARES

A square made of eight lines of dots, eight dots wide, is made on a sheet of paper for each two players. The players take turns drawing lines horizontally or vertically to connect any two dots. The object of the game is to complete a square and to prevent one's opponent from completing any square. Each time a player succeeds in drawing the fourth line of a square he puts his initials in it. The person who finishes a square draws the next line. The one with the most squares containing his initials wins the game.

(Variation: For a progressive party a player scores one point for each completed square and five points extra if he is the winner.)

GUGGENHEIM

Each player draws a chart like the one illustrated, or the charts may be drawn in advance. Any name may be used across the top and a series of four or more nouns is put in the space at the left. The object of the game is to fill in the spaces with words that begin with the letter at the top of the column and are in the class of nouns indicated at the left. For example, if "JANE" is used across the top, and "Cities," "Girls' names," "Boys' names," and "Food" are used on the side, the first line might read, "Juneau," "Annapolis," "New York," "Edinburgh." The second line might read "June," "Alice," "Neva," and "Edna;" the third line could read "Jack," "Arnold," "Nelson," and "Earl;" and the last line "Johnny-cake," "Apples," "Nuts" and "Eggs."

Four points are scored for each entry selected by no one else, and one point for each entry used by other players. The player with the highest score wins.

	J	A	N	E
Cities				
Girls' Names				
Boys' Names				
Foods				

HUMAN TRAITS

Give each player a sheet of paper and pencil and ask him to write as many words as he can which describe the characteristics of teen-agers. Some will immediately list all the good characteristics like honesty, sincerity, and beauty. Others will try to make up a gruesome list. Anyway, it's lots of fun and at the end of fifteen minutes the one with the longest list wins.

LETTER QUIZ

Provide all players with pencils and papers. The leader reads a list of questions which can be answered by a letter or letters. For example, "Containing nothing"—Answer "MT."

		Answers
1.	Statement of indebtedness	O
2.	An insect	B
3.	To behold	C
4.	Part of the body	I
5.	A mournful or plaintive poem	OD
6.	A unit of measure used in printing	M
7.	All right	OK
8.	A slang expression	G
9.	A foe	NME
10.	A vegetable	P
11.	Intemperance	XS
12.	To covet	NV
13.	A bird	J
14.	A beverage	T
15.	A literary effort	SA
16.	A girl's name	B
17.	A residence of diplomats	MBC

The player with the most correct answers wins a prize.

ANIMAL QUIZ

Give each player a pencil and a paper prepared beforehand with a list of animals, fowl, or what-have-you, and the words "Male, female, and offspring" heading three columns opposite each name. The object of the game is to give the correct name applied to the male, female, and offspring of each animal listed. Here is a good list that can be used, with the correct answers already filled in. On the sheets handed out the names for the male, female and offspring will be left blank.

	Male	*Female*	*Offspring*
Deer	Buck	Doe	Fawn
Goat	Billy	Nanny	Kid
Dog	Dog	Bitch	Pup
Donkey	Jack	Jenny	Foal
Fox	Dog	Fox	Vixen
Hog	Boar	Sow	Shoat
Seal	Bull	Cow	Calf
Goose	Gander	Goose	Gosling
Duck	Drake	Duck	Duckling

VIRTUES

This game is good for a family group or for a group the members of which are well-acquainted. Give each player a pencil and paper and remind him that people have good qualities as well as bad. Ask each one to write a trait of character he or she most admires in one of the other players. To remove all restraint the slips should not be signed by the writer. The slips are then collected and the virtues read aloud. It is fun to hear just which traits the crowd most appreciates.

PROGRESSIVE FORTUNES

Each guest is given a sheet of paper and a pencil. Each guest writes his name at the top of the paper and folds it over far enough to conceal the name.

He then passes it to his right-hand neighbor who in turn writes out a four-word description of his own past life. This causes a lot of merriment, especially if it is slightly wicked. The paper is again folded over so that the writing is covered and it is again passed to the right.

Each player then writes a four-word description of the one he or she likes best. After folding over these are passed to the right and each participant states in four words what he thinks of himself.

Once again the papers are folded and passed to the right. Plans for the future are now written in four words by each player, and each paper is passed to the right-hand neighbor who keeps it. Then each player takes turns reading aloud the paper he holds which is supposed to be the fortune of the one whose name appears at the top of the sheet.

SNIFF IT

Fill a dozen small bottles with various liquids such as vinegar, peppermint, ammonia, tea, coffee, water, etc. Each bottle should bear only a number. Each player tries to identify the liquids by smell, writing the number of the bottle and his guess on a card. After each player has had sufficient time to "sniff" and write his answer, the player passes his list to his right-hand partner. When the leader reads the correct list each player corrects the sheet before him. Prize is awarded the most correct list.

ICE

The leader hands out slips of paper with questions on them to be answered with a word containing "ICE." Some suitable questions are:

		Answers
1.	A four-letter ice the world would be better without	Vice
2.	A six-letter ice that occurs three times	Thrice
3.	A five-letter ice fixed by the merchant	Price
4.	A dainty four-letter ice	Nice
5.	A four-letter ice feared by the gals	Mice
6.	A five-letter ice that is cut	Slice
7.	A five-letter ice used in pickles	Spice
8.	A five-letter ice that repeats itself	Twice
9.	A four-letter ice seen at weddings	Rice
10.	A six-letter ice that is easier to give than to take	Advice

NEWS

The leader should tell the players that the newspaper wants a biography of each one. Give each player a list of questions similar to the list below. Each question is to be answered with two words beginning with the writer's first and last initials. Five minutes are allowed for answering questions. Then the answers can be read to the group.

1. Where born?
2. What did father say?
3. Your first words?
4. Favorite sport?
5. Favorite food?
6. Pet peeve?
7. Secret ambition?
8. Type of sweetheart you like?
9. Your opinion of this party?
10. Your opinion of the leader?

PROVERB DRAWING

The leader chooses a familiar proverb without disclosing what he has chosen. For each letter in the proverb he makes an "X" on a child's blackboard or on a large sheet of paper. For instance, "Make hay while the sun shines" would look like this: XXXX XXX XXXXX XXX XXX XXXXX X. Each player draws on a sheet of paper a little outline figure of a man like this:

The first player then says any letter of the alphabet. If he says "A," the leader puts A under the second X in the first word and the second X in the second word. That player is safe for the first round. The second player then announces a letter. If he happens to choose a letter which does not appear in the proverb, then he must erase the head of his man. Then the next player chooses a letter and so on around the circle.

The first time round if a player loses he erases the man's head; the second time he loses he erases the body; the third time, one leg; the fourth time, the second leg; the fifth and sixth times remove the arms.

The game continues and the outline figures diminish until one is completely erased or until some player guesses the proverb. The successful "guesser" wins five points and also the privilege of selecting and writing in "Xs" the next proverb. Ten points are then charged against the loser and each player draws a new man for the next proverb.

8.

Around the World Games

Children the world over skip rope, play hide and seek, and tag. They play much the same games in the far east that we play here. The youngsters of North America enjoy the same fun as the youngsters of South America. Occasionally, one learns of a game that is played specifically in a certain country. Here are a few such games that are adaptable to our own game programs.

DANISH FISH GAME

Players seat themselves in pairs around the room. One couple becomes "It" and is named "Whales." The other couples secretly select the name of a fish. The Whales wander about the room calling out from time to time the name of some fish. The couple whose fish name is called leaves its chairs and marches after the whales. If the whales call out, "The ocean is calm," everyone leaves his chair and follows the whales. When the whales call out, "The ocean is stormy," all the couples race to get chairs. The left-over couple becomes "Whales."

CHINESE DRAGON'S TAIL

Players line up, hands on shoulders of the player ahead. The first player becomes the head of the dragon, the last the tail. The leader calls out "One-two-three-go!" At the signal the head tries to catch the tail. If the head catches the tail, the tail becomes the next head. If the Dragon breaks in two, the one causing the break becomes the tail.

FRENCH SCISSORS GAME

Ahead of time put up four or five rows of string or clothesline. From each clothesline hang twenty penny prizes. Blindfold a player, whirl him around three times, give him a pair of blunt scissors and see how many prizes he can cut down in three minutes. It is against the rules to use the free hand to hang on to the clothesline.

INDIAN CORN

One player hiding kernels of corn in one hand stands before another player in the circle and says, "Guess how many?" He asks his question of each player in the circle. Of course, the one who guesses the correct number of kernels, or the nearest correct, wins and becomes "It" for the next game.

MEXICAN JAR

A novel way to give your party favors is to follow the Mexican Christmas plan of distributing gifts. Instead of a Christmas tree, presents for Mexican children are often put into a clay jar. Christmas Eve the children are blindfolded and with a stick they try to break the jar. When the jar is broken the presents fall on the floor and there is a scramble for the gifts. The one who breaks the jar receives a special gift. So why not, for your party, put your party favors into an inexpensive clay jar and set it on a small table? Let each player in turn be blindfolded and try to break the jar. To him who succeeds in breaking the jar give a special favor.

MEXICAN BREAD AND CHEESE

All players form a circle with the "Buyer" in the center. The Buyer asks one player, "Where do they sell bread and cheese?" That player, Tommy, points to Sally standing at the far side of the ring, and says, "There it is very cheap." The Buyer then goes to Sally and repeats the question. Meanwhile Tommy changes places with Mary who is directly opposite him in the circle. The Buyer then tries to dash into one of the empty spaces before either Tommy or Mary can get there. If the Buyer reaches a vacant spot first, then the one left out becomes the Buyer.

MEXICAN CHARADES

In this game each player acts out some Mexican occupation. For instance: One player carries a jar on her head to show how Mexicans carry water; another dances on the brim of a big sombrero to picture their dances; another weaves a bit of rope to represent the making of twine. Playing a guitar, pottery making, etc., all could be acted out. As each one does his stunt the others guess what he represents.

ALASKAN GUESSING GAME

Players form a circle with "It" in the center. The players all close their eyes while "It" arranges twenty small sticks of wood in a series of groups on the ground. At the signal of "Ready," the players open their eyes and shout out their guess as to the number of sticks on the ground. The one who first guesses the correct number of sticks becomes the next "It." A different number of sticks are used for each time the game is played.

CHINESE GAME

Players sit in a circle. One player puts both hands over his ears. When he does, the player to his right must put his left hand on his left ear, while the player to the left places his right hand on his right ear. (The ear next to the center player alone is covered). The center player suddenly takes both his hands from his ears, and points to some other player in the circle, who immediately puts both hands to his ears. The two players on his right and left assuming the positions described above. The changes are made rapidly and close attention is required. Frequently due to the speed of the action, players make mistakes over which ear to cover, much to the amusement of the crowd.

9.

Musical Games

In any well-rounded recreational activity there's always a demand for a musical game. The music for marches and games can be supplied by phonograph, TV, radio, piano, or even better by group singing. The simplest tune will add zest to the game. For the more music-minded, we offer a few musical paper and pencil games.

DROP A MUSICAL NOTE INTO A TUMBLER

It mystifies your friends to pluck a musical note from the tines of a fork and drop it into an ordinary drinking glass. The trick needs to be done on a bare table. Take the fork in the left hand with the glass near the right hand. Then pick the fork tines with the index and middle fingers of the right hand and quickly place that hand over the open glass and as you do so lower the handle of the fork in your left hand until it touches the table. The fork vibrates when you pick the tines which can be clearly heard as the fork handle touches

the table. Onlookers do not see the handle of the fork
beneath your hand because they are watching your
right hand. It looks as if you were dropping the tone
from the fork into the glass.

DO YOUR EARS HANG LOW?

A musical game that youngsters love is a motion
song. The words are rather silly and the motions even
sillier so naturally it hits the spot. Each player puts
his thumbs to his ears with the fingers free—donkey
fashion. Then all sing to the tune of "Turkey in the
Straw":

Do your ears hang low?—Waggle the fingers

Do they wobble to and fro?—Hands together in
front wave back and forth

Can you tie them in a knot?—Go through motions
of tying a knot

Can you tie them in a bow?—More motions of tying

Can you sling them over your shoulder?—Pretend
to sling folded hands over shoulder

Like a continental soldier?—Salute

Do your ears hang low?—Hands wobbling at ears
again.

The song starts slowly and with each repetition
gets faster and faster, finally ending in a burst of hilarity.

SIAMESE SINGING

Siamese singing is always a riot. It is necessary to
have six or seven copies of the words for this song.

Give them to one group of players and ask them to sing the following words to the tune of "America":

> "O wa ta goo Siam
> O wa ta goo Siam
> O wa ta goos
> O wa ta goo Siam
> O wa ta goo Siam
> O wa ta goo Siam
> O wa ta goos."

It won't take the players long to realize they are singing "Oh, what a goose I am." The other youngsters can then sing the following words, also to the tune of "America":

> "So say we all of us
> Every last one of us
> So say we all
> So say we all of us."

MUSICAL TERMS

For people familiar with common musical terms the following game is entertaining. Players should be supplied with paper and pencils unless it is played orally. Each sentence or phrase can be completed with a musical term.

People live in it	Flat
Used in describing a razor	Sharp
Furniture in a store	Counters
Often passed in school	Notes
A person at ease	Natural
Used in fishing	Lines
What one breathes	Air
A part of a sentence	Phrase
Found on a fish	Scales

Another name for a cane	Staff
Shown by the clock	Time
What we should do at night	Rest
Something for a door	Key
A kind of tar	Pitch

LOOBY LOO

This is a familiar singing game about a pioneer boy's Saturday night bath. One night the fire went out and he had to bathe in cold water. Leader relates the story. Each player represents the boy. (1) All join hands in a circle and skip to left, repeating this after each verse of pantomime. (2) Pantomime, stand facing center, put right hand in toward center, gingerly; snatch it out, shake it vigorously and turn in place. Repeat as indicated by words of succeeding verses. On last verse all jump into center, out again, shake themselves, turn and finish with a hand-clap or whoop.

1. Chorus

    Here we go Loo - by Loo, —
Here we go Loo - by, light
    Here we go Loo - by Loo —
all on a Sat - ur - day night

2.

    I put my right hand in — I
put my right hand out — I
give my right hand a shake, shake
shake, and turn my self about, Oh,

2. I put my left hand in, etc. 5. I put my left foot in, etc.

3. I put my two hands in, etc. 6. I put my head way in, etc.

4. I put my right foot in, etc. 7. I put my whole self in, etc.

THE OLD GREY MARE

Music: First part of "The Old Grey Mare" sung first time very slowly, repeated very quickly.

Words: The old grey mare, she
Ain't what she used to be
Ain't what she used to be
Ain't what she used to be
The old grey mare, she
Ain't what she used to be
Many long years a-
Go - o - O!

Formation: In three's (two women with man in center or vice versa), arms linked, moving forward zig zag, three abreast, counterclockwise in a large circle.

Action: Part 1. Very slowly move diagonally right forward, starting right foot, three slow steps and kick to the words "The old (step) grey (step) mare (step) she (kick)." Repeat, starting left foot, moving diagonally left forward on second line, "Ain't (step) what (step) she used to (step) be (kick)." Repeat all, three more times. Part 2. Release arms, man faces woman on his right and links arms with her, turning her quickly on first line, links left arms with woman on left, turning her quickly on second line and so on to end of song when man moves forward to join a new pair of ladies.

Method of   Continue indefinitely playing Part 1 slower and
Play: slower, Part 2 faster and faster.

WORKIN' ON THE RAILROAD

Formation: Couples face counterclockwise, man with his partner to his right. March in circle, holding hands. Music of familiar song ("Levee Song").

Action: March counterclockwise on the first line and
            stop. On the second line standing in place, put
            the left foot forward, heel to the floor, withdraw
            it, then right foot forward, withdraw it. On
            third beat bend the knees slightly. On fourth
            beat raise the partner's hand, look her in the
            eye, and say, "Hey!" March again for third line
            and step in place for fourth. March again for
            fifth and step in place for sixth. March again
            for seventh and step in place for eight except
            on the eighth line which is "Dinah, blow your
            horn," you do not say "Hey!" but "Toot Toot!"
            On "Toot! Toot!" players let go of hands and
            boys move ahead one girl for a new partner
            and the game is repeated as long as desired.

MAGIC MUSIC

Send someone out of the room and hide some article
on a person with only a small part of it showing. When
the searcher returns have everyone sing a popular song.
The nearer he gets to the article, the louder the music
is. The farther away he gets, the softer the music is.
The one on whom the article is found must leave the
room next.

Variation: Article may be hidden anywhere in the
room and then the finder chooses one to go out.

O SUSANNA

Words: 1. I came to Alabama wid my banjo on my knee,
          2. I'm gwan to Louisiana, my true love for to see.
          3. It rained all night de day I left,
             De weather it was dry,
             De sun so hot I froze to death,
             Susanna don't you cry.

Chorus: 4. O Susanna, Oh, don't you cry for me,
              For I goin' to Louisiana, wid my banjo on my
              knee.

Formation: Single circle, by partners, all facing the center
Action: (1) Drop hands. Ladies walk four steps to cen-
             ter, and back to place. (2) Men the same. (3)
             Grand right and left. Partners join right hands
             and pass each other by right shoulders, men
             moving counterclockwise, ladies clockwise. Con-
             tinue in the same direction, alternately taking
             left and right hands, weaving in and out. Count-
             ing original partner as No. 1, each will take the
             seventh person he meets as his new partner. (4)
             On the chorus, each man gets a new partner, and
             joining hands in skating position, they prome-
             nade counterclockwise. Come into a single cir-
             cle at the end, and repeat as often as desired.

SINGING PROVERBS

Divide the players into two or more small groups.
Each small group goes to a special place in the room
and decides upon a proverb. Then each member of
the group chooses a different word of the proverb
which he is to sing steadily to the tune of Dixie. If
there are more players in the group than words in the
proverb, two or more players take the same word.

The other groups listen to the "concert." The first
of the listening groups to correctly guess the proverb
gets the next opportunity to sing its proverb.

PLATTER FUN

Here's a musical game that's fun for smaller groups. Give each player a paper and pencil. Have on hand about twelve records.

Play the first record. Each person must name selection, orchestra and singer. Five points are given for the correct title, three points for the name of the orchestra and two points for the name of the singer. In other words it is possible to get ten points for each record.

When all twelve records are played, scores are added, and the one with the most points gets her choice of record.

SONG SINGING

For a musical crowd nothing is more fun than this game. As he arrives each person is given the name of a song to sing. He must sing his song as he goes about the room finding the group who is singing the same song. This is an excellent way to divide a big crowd into smaller groups for the evening.

MUSICAL MARCHING

This is a good mixer. The girls form a small circle, and the boys form a larger circle outside them. A good marching tune or a song that everybody can sing is started, and everybody marches to the right. On a signal the boys about face while the girls keep on marching to the right. When the signal is given again, the boys grab partners and march with the girls in the direction which the girls are going.

10.

Games for Small Spaces

GOING OUT TO DINNER

Two people who know this game should start it. For instance, John Jessup and Mary White might start it off. Mary might say, "I'm going out to dinner and bring back More Watermelons. What are you bringing back, John?" John could answer, "I'm going out to dinner and bring back Just Jugs." Then John calls on someone else who probably will fail to bring back the right thing. This can be continued until the crowd catches on that the articles brought back begin with the initials of the first and last names of the person talking.

SARDINES

One player is "It" and hides in a roomy place. Then all quietly hunt for him. As soon as one finds "It" he hides with him. This goes on until all the players are packed like sardines in one place. It is hard for the hidden ones to keep from laughing as the others hunt.

BLOCKS

This game is played with children's blocks which bear a letter on each of the six surfaces. The players take turns in rolling the blocks. The object is to see how many words can be made from the letters that turn up. No letter can be used more than once, but it isn't necessary to use all the letters each time. For example, when H.A.A.S.E.T. comes up, the thrower can make at least nine words, AS, TEA, HAT, SAT, SET, HAS, HEAT, THE, and ASH. Each player keeps his own score, giving himself one point for each word that can be made from the letters that come up.

To make this into a Valentine game, award the player ten points if "Hearts" can be spelled.

ADJECTIVES

The leader gives each player a slip of paper and asks him to write an adjective on the slip and sign his name. The leader then collects the slips and makes up a story using the player's name and his own descriptive adjective. For instance, the leader might say **"Vicious** Tom Brown went walking one day and whom should he see but **gangling** Bill Shaw."

This game is particularly funny because much of the time the unwitting player chooses an adjective most inappropriate; the fat guest choosing "skinny" and the thin one "enormous."

ALMOST BUT NOT QUITE BIRTHDAY PARTY

(Good for 6th, 7th, and 8th graders)

This party is for everybody's birthday. Each player has been asked to bring from home a white elephant gift. The gifts are numbered and then numbers are drawn from a hat. Someone draws the numbers from the hat and another passes out the gifts. It is fun to give prizes to the best wrapped package, the funniest gift, the most unusual gift, and the most appropriate.

In case someone, or several, do actually have birthdays during the month, cupcakes with a single candle can be served.

FAMILY TIES

The next time you have a family get-together, ask each male to bring one or two discarded ties. Every man has a few dozen or so which he hangs on to "just in case." Put all the neckties in one basket with the guests seated around the room. The game is to let the rest of the family guess the owner. As each tie is held up for inspection it is greeted with a running fire of comment as to the type of tie it is and what inner urge might make a man buy it. The first person guessing the owner correctly will be awarded the tie.

THE CAPITAL

This game calls for a large map of the United States to be put on the wall. Give each player an American flag sticker on which he writes his own initials. Players take turns being blindfolded and spun about. Then each tries to stick his flag on Washington, D.C. The one whose flag lands nearest its goal receives a prize. For a Washington party, the prize can be a sack of cherries.

PANTOMINE RHYMES

The leader says, "I'm thinking of a word that rhymes with _____" (using a single syllable word.) Anyone in the circle may respond by saying, "Is it _____ then pantomine a word. For example, the leader thinks of the word "Clock" and says "I'm thinking of a word that rhymes with "rock." One person may pantomine "knock" and go through the motions of knocking at the door. The leader says, "No, it is not knock." Another pantomines setting the clock and the leader says, "Yes, it is 'clock.' " Person guessing "clock" starts game again.

CORK SNAP

Place a pop bottle on the corner of a table with a cork or marshmallow on top of bottle. Each player starts from a line ten feet from the table and walks rapidly toward the bottle with arm outstretched and hand in position for snapping the cork off the top of the bottle. That is, the hand is held palm down with the middle finger touching the thumb. Player must not hesitate in his progress toward the bottle. It is surprising to see how few will snap off the cork.

II.

Stunts

FANCY STEPPING

A group of guests, who do not know the stunt, are assembled in one room. In another room the leader places four objects a little distance apart across the living room floor. Good things to use are a whole raw egg, a plant, a cut glass vase, and a silver teapot—the more fragile the things the better. Then one "victim" is brought into the room and told that he will be blindfolded and will have to step over the fragile objects without touching them. To help him gauge the distance, permit him to step over the articles with his eyes open. Much atmosphere is created by repeated cautionings as to the value and fragility of the objects. The victim is then blindfolded, spun around three times and started on his perilous course. While he is being spun the objects are quietly removed from the floor. The victim then starts out working diligently to step over the things that are no longer there. It is terrifically funny to watch people stepping high, wide, and handsome over a bare spot on the floor. The game is repeated until all the uninformed victims from the outer room have had a chance to try their skill.

MAGIC RINGS

The magician shows three paper rings of identical size which he hangs over his left arm. He tells the group these are magic Hindu rings. "As you see they are all the same size but I will cut them in such a way that one will become two rings, another will be one long ring, and the third will make two linking rings."

He then takes the first ring from his arm and cuts around the ring as near the center as possible. This makes two complete rings; all very simple and easy to understand.

The second ring he removes from his arm and cuts exactly as he did the first but it makes one long ring. The last ring he cuts exactly in the same way as the others but it turns out to be a ring within a ring.

The explanation is the way the original rings are made. Using ordinary funny paper so as to have bright-colored rings, cut three strips four inches wide the full length of the longest way of the newspaper. Then paste two ends of one strip together the flat way—that is, when the ends are pasted together it makes a plain circle or ring. This is the ring that makes two plain rings when cut.

For the second ring—the one that turns into one long ring when cut—make one turn in the paper before pasting the ends together flatwise.

For the third ring—the one that makes a ring within a ring—make a double twist in the paper before pasting together. When the rings are hung over the magician's arm the twists in the paper are not noticeable.

SECRET FORTUNES

Beforehand write some fortunes with secret ink on pieces of white paper. To do this dissolve one tablespoonful of common table salt in one-half cup of water and write with a clean stub point pen. In writing with secret ink dip the pen frequently. Then before the writing dries draw a black pencil line under the fortune to indicate the location of the sentence on the paper. Have the writing dry thoroughly before laying the papers together.

Hand a sheet to each player and ask him to press his thumb on an ink pad and then on the paper. Thus each player fingerprints his own fortune. Explain that each sheet has a fortune that can be found with a pencil. It won't take the player long to discover that words will appear by rubbing the pencil lightly over the paper. Here are some fortunes that are fun.

1. Don't get killed in the dark of the moon—it's fatal.

2. You'll soon be dead—dead wrong.

3. Don't watch the clock so much—it may strike.

4. It's unlucky for you to drown on Friday the 13th.

5. Don't cultivate a taking way—your friends may miss things.

6. Your rich relatives will soon leave you—but they won't leave you much.

7. If you're searching for a clue, look under "c" in the dictionary.

8. Never take a job on the 32nd day of the month.

EGG IN THE BOTTLE

Equipment: a peeled hard-boiled egg
quart milk bottle
match

This stunt is not new, but it's always fun and surprising for each new group that tries it. Each player is given an empty milk bottle, clean, of course, with the request that he put a peeled egg into his bottle. The peeled egg is larger than the top of the bottle. The player can push and squeeze on the slippery eggs but he'll make no progress. Then the leader (who knows the trick) lights a match, drops it in the bottle. He places the egg on the mouth of the empty bottle and the egg will slowly slide into the bottle.

The explanation is that the lighted match in the bottle uses up the oxygen in the bottle, thereby creating a partial vacuum. Then the outside air pressure forces the egg into the bottle.

To get the egg out of the bottle is something else again. With all the shaking, jiggling, and jouncing the egg will not come out. Once again the leader can show the way. Simply turn the bottle upside down and blow into it. The pressure of air will then force the egg out of the bottle. This is a good stunt that all the players will want to try.

SHIRT REMOVAL

This is a stunt where one of the players acts as a magician. His stunt is to remove a man's or boy's shirt from him **without** removing his coat. Seat the man on a chair in full sight. The magician then eyes the seated man and says, "I don't like the way your collar buttons." With that he unbuttons his shirt collar and a couple of buttons down the front of the shirt.

Then the magician further criticizes, "These are funny cuffs." He reaches down and unbuttons the shirt cuffs. Finally the magician says, "I don't like the looks of your shirt at all." Firmly gripping the man's shirt by the back of the collar, he tugs a bit. The shirt will then come off without the man's coat being unbuttoned.

The secret is that the man having his shirt removed must be in on the stunt. He lets his shirt hang down his back. By buttoning the collar and a couple of buttons down the front and buttoning the cuffs around his wrists, the shirt appears to be on when he is wearing a coat. When the magician unbuttons these few buttons it is a simple matter to pull the shirt from under the man's coat. But it does look very mysterious.

THE TEASER

Here's a stunt that is a teaser. Explain to your guests that each one must stand with his heels close against the wall behind him and place a coin on the floor in front of him just eighteen inches from his toes.

Winners are the ones who can pick up the coins in front of them without losing their balance.

MAGIC STICK

The players are told that if they touch the magic stick it will prevent them from walking straight across the room, picking up a book from the floor, and placing it on a chair standing in one corner of the room. Usually the group is skeptical. Choose the loudest skeptic to make the first try.

Tell him to stand in the center of the floor with his hands cupped over the head of the cane (yardstick) and lean his forehead on his hands. Watching the end of the cane on the floor, he circles six times. Then he drops the stick and tries to walk across the room toward the book. Chances are he'll zig when he means to zag, and will land in a heap on the floor. This is fun to watch and usually players are anxious to try their turn to see if they can do it without staggering.

NINE TOOTHPICKS

Each player is given five toothpicks. Then the leader offers six more to anyone who can make them into nine toothpicks. All eleven toothpicks must be used. This is quite a puzzle until someone discovers that by laying the toothpicks so as to make the word N I N E he has used all eleven toothpicks.

INDIAN WEDDING

This ceremony is most fun with a small group of boys.

1. Boys stand shoulder to shoulder, facing the front.
2. All raise hands above the head.
3. Bend to kneeling position, keeping the knees tightly together.
4. Put hands behind the back and clasp firmly.
5. Bend over and put forehead on the floor.

As soon as all the boys are in this position, the leader gives the lad at the end a stiff nudge, whereupon the whole group topples over on their sides like dominos. The kneeling position assures no one will be hurt and boys greatly enjoy this game.

BROOMSTICK BALANCE

Make a bridge by laying a broomstick on the seats of two chairs a slight distance apart. With the aid of a cane the contestant seats himself on the broomstick and crosses his legs. When he is nicely balanced he endeavors to remove with his cane two handkerchiefs that are hung on the back of the chair behind him. Three falls are allowed before he is declared a loser, and given another try.

HAT PASSING

Players stand in a circle, each with a hat on his or her head, with his right hand on the hat of the person next to him. When the music starts each player removes his right hand neighbor's hat and puts it on his own head. The faster the music plays the faster goes the exchange of hats. When the music stops, the action stops. When it starts again the players do the same thing in the opposite direction. (Left hand on head of player at left). This is especially funny if at the start the men wear women's hats and the women wear men's hats.

AIR LIFT

This stunt has been passed from generation to generation. Victim is asked to stand on a stout board with her hand on the heads of persons on either side. She is then blindfolded and told that she will be raised off the floor. People at either end raise the board a small distance off the floor while the persons on either side slowly stoop down, thus giving the victim the illusion that she is going much higher than she really is. She is then asked to jump. A ridiculous performance to watch.

I SEE A B'AR

Players line up in a row, side by side, shoulders touching, facing the same direction. Leader is the first in line. Turning to the person next to him, he says, "I see a B'ar." The next person says, "Wh'ar?" "Thar," answers the leader pointing straight ahead of him with his right arm. This procedure is followed on down the line until it reaches the last person. The leader starts again, this time pointing straight ahead with his left arm. The third time he stoops and points with his right foot. When everyone is in this precarious position, the leader repeats for the last time, "I see a b'ar" and on the word, "Thar," he knocks over the person next to him which results in everyone going down like a pack of dominoes. A truly hilarious game.

12.

Games With Balls
or Other Equipment

Ball games appeal to all ages and can be used in small play spaces or in open recreation fields. We offer here a group of games calling for a ball or other small equipment.

BEACH BALL

Players form a circle and number 1, 2, 1, 2, and so on around the circle. The players numbered 1 become one team and are given a blue beach ball; those numbered 2 are the opposing team and are given a red ball. The balls are passed to team members only. This means that each player throws the ball past the person standing next to him and into the hands of his own teammate immediately beyond.

At a signal the balls are started off in opposite directions. The balls have to make three complete trips around the circle to finish one race. The balls change directions after each race; that is, the team of players after passing its ball three times around to the right for the first race, pass it three times around to the left for the second race, and around to the right again for the last. The team winning two out of three races is champion. Large colored balloons can be substituted for beach balls.

FAN BALL

> Equipment: Two ping pong balls
>   Heavy pieces of cardboard for fans

The players line up in two straight rows facing each other. Draw a chalk line in front of their toes. (Chalk will vacuum off a rug with no trouble.) Give each player a heavy piece of cardboard to be used as a fan. Toss two ping-pong balls between the two rows of players. The object of the game is for each team to fan the ball over the opponents' line. The players must stay behind the lines. The balls can't be touched—only fanned. A referee keeps track of the scores and announces the winners. The action of these elusive little balls makes this a really exciting game.

UMBRELLA BALL

Open a small umbrella or parasol and put it upside down in the center of the room. The smaller the umbrella the better. The players circle around the umbrella about three feet from it. Each player takes a turn at tossing the ball into an open umbrella. If the ball stays in, the player wins one point. For this game it is best to use a hard ball like a golf ball, because it bounces in and out more readily. A ping pong ball or some such light ball stays put too well to make the game exciting.

RING PAN TOSS

Equipment: angel-food tin and 5 ping pong balls

Set an angel-food cake tin on a table. Stick an adhesive tape marked "5" on the outer ring of the pan, and a tape marked "25" on the inner ring. Players use five ping pong balls for the game. Standing at the opposite end of the table from the cake tin, they bounce the balls into the pan. Balls falling into the outer ring earn five points and inner ring twenty-five points. Captain keeps track of scores and announces winners.

BASEMENT BOWLING

Set ten tin cans in ten-pin formation. Use croquet balls for bowling balls. Give one point for every ten-pin knocked over and fifteen if all the cans fall at one shot.

BOUNCE

Place a wastebasket on a chair some distance from the wall. Mark a line about six feet back from the chair on which the player stands. The game is to bounce the ball on the floor so that it goes into the basket. Each one has three tries, as this is not as easy to do as it seems. A point is given for every basket made. After a given length of time points are counted to determine the winner.

LASSO

Equipment: small clothesline lasso and cowboy hat

Hang the hat on the back of a chair. Try to lasso the hat off the chair from a distance of ten feet. Each player is given three tries. An extra try is given for a successful throw.

CLOCK GOLF

Draw a circle fifteen feet in diameter and number it around its circumference like a clock face. Place a tin can, about four inches in diameter, in the center of the circle. So that the balls will roll into the can, fit a wide sloping cardboard collar around the can.

The players take positions at the numbers on the clock face. Each player has a golf stick and tries to put the golf ball in the can. The winner is the one who "holes out" in the smallest number of strokes.

WALL BALL

Players number off and scatter about. Number one player tosses the ball against a wall and, after the ball leaves his hand, calls a number. The player whose number is called has to catch the ball on the first bounce. If he is successful in catching the ball, he throws it and calls a number. If he doesn't catch the ball on the first bounce, the original thrower throws it again.

13.

Games for Special Days

No one ever needs an excuse for fun. But the special days in our calendar seem to issue invitations to throw a party or a get-together. Almost any game can be adapted to a holiday party, but just to get your thinking-cap to working well, here are a suggested few. You can take it from here.

Valentine Day Games

SWEET READING

Players are divided into two groups of equal number. The groups stand at opposite sides of the room. The leader of each group is given an envelope containing three valentines, each of which bears a four-line verse. At the starting signal the leader takes the valentines out of the envelope one by one, reads them aloud, puts them back into the envelope and hands the envelope to the next player. As both groups read valentines aloud at the same time, the noise is hilarious. The first group to get the valentines read wins the game.

HEART STORY

Each player receives a dozen candy hearts—the kind that bears a sentimental or slang expression. A prize is offered to the one making the most complete sentence from the words on the hearts. The result is that players trade furiously until they get candies with expressions that fit together. This is lively entertainment.

HEART HUNT

Ahead of time hide dozens of small red hearts made of construction paper in every conceivable place around the game room. The players pair off in teams and join hands. The hunt begins while someone plays the piano or a record player. The players hunt fast and furiously, as long as the music continues. When the music stops, the players stop in their tracks. If anyone moves after the music stops, or if he drops his partner's hands while hunting, he is disqualified. The team finding the most hearts wins the game.

HEARTY WORDS

Group is divided into couples. Each couple is given a paper and pencil. The object of the game is to build as many words as possible from the letters in the word "Valentine," using a letter in a word only as many times as it appears in the original word, "Valentine." The couple with the longest list wins the prize. Better have a dictionary handy to settle arguments over spelling, etc.

HEART SURRENDER

Each player is given ten small hearts (made from red construction paper). Players are allowed fifteen minutes in which to go around the room talking to one another. Every time anyone uses the words "I," "me," or "you," he must surrender a heart to the one who catches him at it. Each person tries to get as many hearts as possible while surrendering as few as possible. Those losing all their hearts must pay a forfeit, decided upon by the one acquiring the most hearts.

TELEGRAMS

Supply each guest with pencil and paper and ask them to write telegrams using only nine words beginning with the letters of "Valentine." As for instance, "Valor alters love. Even now thine is not enough." Allow ten minutes for composition of telegrams. Then collect them and read them aloud. Prizes can be awarded to the one making the most sense, the "corniest," and the most beautiful.

Variation: This game can be adapted to any holiday by substituting the appropriate word, such as Christmas, Thanksgiving, Easter, etc., in place of Valentine.

HEART SNIP

On a line strung across the room hang a number of red cardboard hearts that have been tied on strings of varying length. Players work in couples. One is blindfolded and the partner tries to steer the blindfolded player to the hearts by a short piece of string fastened to the blindfolded one's wrist. The partner can say nothing but must direct with small tugs at the string. The team snipping down the most hearts wins the game.

PAN THE HEARTS

Divide the crowd into two groups, each of which forms a circle. In the center of each circle put a large pie tin on the floor. Sprinkle tissue paper hearts around it. Give each player a paper plate to be used for a fan. At a signal everyone fans with the plate, trying to blow the hearts into the pie tins. This game is hilarious because the harder the fanning the higher the hearts fly. And they blow out of the pie tin almost easier than they blow in. The team with the most hearts in the pan after ten windy minutes wins the game.

St. Patrick's Day

PIG IN THE PARLOR

The group, with the exception of one person, forms a double circle—boys in the outer circle, girls in the inner. The one person becomes "Pig" in the center of the circle. Everybody marches to the following words (tune: "We won't be home until morning"):

> Got a pig in the parlor
> Got a pig in the parlor
> Got a pig in the parlor,
> And he is Irish too
> And he is Irish too
> And he is Irish too,
> Got a pig in the parlor
> Got a pig in the parlor
> Got a pig in the parlor
> And he is Irish too.

The girls continue marching in the same direction in which they are going while the men turn about and go in the opposite direction. When this change is made the "pig" from the center joins the circle. The leader blows the whistle, and there is a scramble for new partners. One is bound to be left out and he now becomes the "pig." After several scrambles for partners the ice is pretty well broken and the whistle sounds for a change of game.

IRISH GOLF

Each group is given a large bowl, an Irish potato and a tablespoon. The object is to scoop the potato into the bowl with the spoon without lifting it from the table. Add the strokes it takes each member of the group to get the potato into the bowl. To the winning group who accomplishes it with the least number of strokes goes an Irish potato.

Fourth of July Games

BOMBS

Divide your guests into two groups of equal number. The two teams line up facing each other, about eight or ten feet apart. Give each player a toy balloon and when the game starts, the player at the head of each line must inflate his balloon until it bursts. The next in line then does the same, and so on down the line. No cheating is allowed. The second player must wait to blow up his balloon until the first player's balloon has popped. The group first popping all its balloons wins.

FIND THE FLAG

Ask one player to leave the room. Then hide an American flag, so that the entire crowd except the absent member knows where it is. Call back the player and explain to him that while he hunts the flag the crowd is going to sing "Yankee Doodle"—softly when he is far from it, louder as he nears it, and very loud when he gets it. This is a lively game—each one will want his turn at finding the flag.

Halloween

HALLOWEEN GHOST STORY

A ghost story in which the guests take parts of story characters is always popular. Suitable ghost stories to be read or told can be found in any library such as W. B. Holland's Twenty-five Ghost Stories; Washington Irving's Bold Dragon and other tales; Montague Rhodes James' Collected Ghost Stories; and Ethel Owen's Halloween Tales and Games. Assign each character in the story chosen to a guest. When the story teller mentions a character the one representing it dramatizes the part.

For instance, in one Halloween romance there are eight characters. When the story mentions, "Sweet young thing," the one having that part says "Tee, hee, hee," the "Strong young chap" sings a bar of "Sweet

Mystery of Life," the "canary in the cage" says "Twitter, twitter;" the "cat on the hearth," "Prrow;" "Dark and stormy nights, "Hoo-oo-oo;" "Dying dogs," "Ki-yi;" "Cruel old father," "Gr-humph;" and "Gray ghosts," "Ooooooooooh."

BLACK CAT RELAY

Before the party cut out of black construction paper two large cardboard cats. Run a string about twelve feet long through the head of each cat. Tie one end of each string to a chair across the room high enough from the floor so that each cat stands on its hind legs. Divide the players into two teams. Give the captains of each team the loose ends of the strings and tell them to move the cats by jerking the strings across the room and to the operator of the string. The next man in line jerks the cat back up to the chair. Of course, the first team through wins the race.

GHOSTLY HALLOWEEN LIGHTS

Place three or four lighted candles in the middle of the floor. Seat your guests in a circle on the floor and have someone tell a ghost story. As the storytelling proceeds, the candles will go out one by one until at last all the candles are out. It is very spooky.

The secret of this stunt is to cut the candles in two. By heating the pieces slightly they may be put together again until the candles look like new. When lighted the candle will burn until it reaches the cut wick. By cutting the candles at various lengths, they will go out one by one as the spooky story progresses.

APPLE GRAB

For a variation of "Apple Bob" tie apples to strings hung in an open doorway. A contestant with hands behind his back tries for a bite at the swinging apple. In a large archway there is room for five or six apples hung side by side. It is loads of fun for the onlookers to watch the struggling contestants.

CAT RELAY

Players are divided into two teams. Each player, for the moment becomes a Halloween cat, and is given a saucer of milk. At the word "Meow," cats start lapping. (Did you ever lap milk? It's pretty funny.) Team that licks the saucers clean first, wins and can be dubbed the "Cat's Whiskers."

CAT GAME

The Cat Game will give your guests a real thrill. It's a must at your family parties on Halloween night. All lights are dimmed. Big and little guests sit on the floor in a circle, a sheet spread in the center. Each one takes hold of the sheet with his left hand and keeps his right hand free under the sheet. The hostess appears holding a tray covered with a napkin and says in a solemn voice:

"This evening when the Halloween cat was on the way to our party it was run over. His remains will now be passed around under the sheet. This is the cat's eye —just pass it to your neighbor and so on around the circle **under the sheet.**" The hostess reaches under the sheet to hand the first person an icy oyster, to be followed by the head—a ball of yarn filled with hairpins; tail—a coon tail from a child's cap; teeth—a string of large beads, chilled; hide—a brushed wool helmet; tongue—a very cold watermelon pickle; insides—a bunch of soft dough, well-floured. The shrieks accompanying this game are hair-raising.

HALLOWEEN BROOMSTICKS

The players are divided into two groups. Each player has a bit of toothpick. Occasionally a whole toothpick is handed out to add impetus. The captains from each line race across the room and lay their toothpicks on the table. The second players lay their toothpicks next to their captain's. The object of the game is to see which team can lay the longest broomstick (toothpicks laid end to end) at the end of ten minutes.

FORTUNE TELLING DREAMS

No Halloween party is complete without a fortune telling stunt. Beforehand have a girl prepared to be your gypsy fortune teller. Under an umbrella canopy you can make a realistic-looking fire by laying a few sticks across orange tissue paper with flashlights concealed underneath. Burning incense gives the effect of steam issuing forth. Instruct the fortune teller to question each one about his last dream. She can interpret these dreams according to the following meanings. If you pick a clever gypsy, she can also use her imagination and her knowledge of the client to make the fortunes particularly apt. Some common interpretations of dreams are:

Snakes—deceitful enemies
Lightning—beware of accidents
Falling—beware of money losses, hard times
Crying—joy
Sunset—love affair
Fog—end of your troubles is coming
Writing—will receive an important letter
Laughing—love or business disappointment
Suffering—wealth
Flames—gossip
Black cat or crows—bad news
Riding on train—visitors
Hungry—plenty
Fighting—success in love, prosperity
Strange faces—travel

WITCH'S BREW

Suspend a large iron kettle over a make-believe fire. It will appear to be just a part of the decoration. Just about the time all guests have forgotten about it, a witch rushes into the room. In a covered basket she has a number of ingredients which are needed for charms. She hands the basket to the hostess and retires to her kettle, muttering.

Each player is then blindfolded and a line is formed. The hostess then explains that all the objects which are in the basket must be passed from guest to guest in the line and finally handed to the witch. The first article can be a hot baked potato, which passes quickly from hand to hand amidst sudden exclamations of various kinds. A chestnut burr can be next, followed by a piece of ice, an old glove filled with mush, a large soup bone, a large peeled grape and an oyster.

The blindfolded guests will emit bloodcurdling shrieks as the objects touch their hands. At the end of the line the objects are placed in a kettle and stirred vigorously by the witch while the guests, blindfolds removed, look into the kettle. When all ingredients are thoroughly stirred the witch takes from the kettle a written fortune for each guest.

RING THE BELL

For this relay divide the players into two teams. Hang in an open doorway a big orange-colored cardboard pumpkin with a large opening in one side. Suspend a small bell inside the pumpkin. Give the first player on each team a bean bag and tell him to ring the bell. Each player has one try and then passes the bean bag to the next player. A scorekeeper reports on which team rings the bell the greater number of times.

WITCH HUNT

A good way to start a Halloween party off is to tell the guests that you have just heard that two witches have come to town and that you suspect they are among the guests; that they must be caught immediately before they can do horrible damage. (Two of the guests have agreed beforehand to be the witches.) The hostess describes the two witches as to height, weight, color of hair and eyes, habits, etc., and adds, if she sees fit, humorous comments. The guests immediately hunt for the two witches that have just been described. As soon as someone believes he has spotted one of the witches he extends his hand and reads in a loud voice from a card (which has previously been given each guest by the hostess) the following:

> When shall we meet again?
> Thunder, lightning or in rain?
> Better take it on the lam,
> Old black witch, beat it, scram.

If he has pointed out the real witch, the witch disappears rapidly through the nearest door. If the discoverer is wrong, he gets a Bronx cheer for his efforts. The game ends when both witches have been discovered and sent out.

HALLOWEEN HAGS

Draw on a sheet a life-size witch with stringy hair, peaked hat, etc., with a hole where the face should be seen. Hang a sheet in an open doorway. Let the girls stick their heads in the opening, making faces to disguise their identities. Boys write their guesses as to whom each one is. Then the girls take their turns at guessing whose face they see. It is surprising how hard it is to guess each face.

YARN OF THE FUTURE

Everyone likes to have his fortune told. For this fortune game prepare beforehand by tying a written fortune every two feet on a ball of yarn. Then rewind the ball, adding extra yarn so the paper fortunes won't show. The leader tosses the ball to a player who unwinds until he comes to the first paper. He removes the paper and then tosses the ball to someone else. This continues until each player has a paper. Then the players take turns reading aloud. Here are some fortune suggestions that are fun:

1. Never get married on the 32nd day of the month.
2. Don't get killed in the dark of the moon—it's fatal.
3. You'll soon be dead—dead wrong.
4. Don't watch the clock so closely—it may strike.
5. It's unlucky for you to drown on Friday the 13th.
6. You'll shine in society—if you don't powder your nose.
7. Don't cultivate a taking way—your friends may miss things.
8. Beware of courtships—they often sink.
9. Your rich relatives will soon leave you—but they won't leave you much.
10. If you're looking for love, see "l" in the dictionary.

PUMPKIN SEEDS

Players are seated in a circle on the floor with a bowl of slippery pumpkin seeds in the center. Each player is given a needle and thread. At a given signal the players all begin to string the slippery pumpkin seeds. At the end of ten minutes a prize is given the player with the most seeds on his string.

PUMPKIN SEED RELAY

(Variation of "Pumpkin Seeds")

Divide the group into couples. Give each lady a

cup of wet pumpkin seeds and supply each man with a threaded needle. As each lady hands the man a seed from her supply, he threads it on a needle and runs it down the thread. If he drops the seed, he must recover it before another seed can be threaded. The couple finishing the cup of seeds first wins the game.

BITE THE APPLE

Hang a string from the center of a doorway. On it fasten a short stick or cane so that it remains parallel to the floor. From one end of the stick suspend a ripe juicy apple. Spin the cane merry-go-round fashion as fast as possible. Then let the first brave soul step close and try to bite the apple as it flies past. If he succeeds in biting the apple, he will be, or is, lucky in matters of love. If he fails, he's very unlucky and will need considerable dusting off.

CANDLE BLOW

Line up seven lighted candles on the table. Ask a guest to stand six or eight feet from the table facing the candles. Blindfold him and turn him completely around three times. Then tell him to walk to the table and blow three times at the candle flames. Allow him three blows and no more. If he blows out all the candles he will be rich this year. If he fails to blow out any, he'll be poor all his life. If 1, 2, 3, 4, 5, or 6 candles are left burning they indicate the number of years before he will become rich.

INITIAL FORTUNES

Each player is equipped with a pencil and paper, and writes his own initials at the top of the page. The leader collects the papers and then redistributes them so no one gets his own. Then each player, using the initials he finds at the top of his sheet, answers the following questions as the leader reads them aloud. Suppose the initials were M. W.; the answers might be like this:

	Answers
1. Of what does he or she remind you?	More watermelon
2. How old does he or she look	Much worn
3. What can he or she do best?	Manhandle women
4. What is his or her chief wickedness?	Munching worms
5. What is his or her chief hobby?	Making work
6. What will his or her work be?	Mainly worrying

The papers are returned to the original owners and each in turn reads his fortune aloud.

NUT FORTUNES

Beforehand remove peanuts or walnuts from their shells. Insert tiny folded bits of paper on which are written such words as "Journey," "Wealth," "Success," "Five children," "Two husbands," "Three wives," "Hard work." Hide them around the room. Announce that somewhere in the room is a peanut with a fortune inside. Each player must hunt until he finds one. After everyone has a peanut, ask the players to open the shells and read their fortunes. Providing only one apiece eliminates that scramble that usually accompanies an indoor hunt.

HALLOWEEN HUNT

Players are divided into three or four groups, depending upon the number of contestants. Each group chooses its own leader. Each leader is provided with a string on which to put paper pumpkins when found. Each group chooses a signal such as barking, meowing, or crowing. No one except the leader is allowed to pick up a pumpkin. When one of the players finds a pumpkin he places his finger on it and barks, or meows, or crows, or what his group is supposed to do until the leader comes to pick it up. The group, whose leader has the longest string of pumpkins, wins.

SPIDER

Upon arrival each guest is given a large spool and one end of a string. These strings should be arranged so that they cross each other and wind here and there about the room beneath carpets, around chair rungs and behind pictures. All lead to one large black cardboard spider hanging in the center of the room. At a given signal everyone begins winding. The winner is the one who reaches the spider first with all his string wound on his spool. He is then given the spider as a prize.

GOBLET FORTUNES

Place a goblet on a table. Tie a ring to a string. Let each player drop the ring to the bottom of the goblet while he recites the alphabet. Immediately when the ring strikes the side of the goblet the player stops. The letter with which he or she stops is indication of the name of the person he or she will marry.

CHEW IT

Tie candy pumpkins or orange or black jelly beans to a string. Make each string about three feet long. Instruct each guest to put the free end of the string into his mouth and hold his hands behind his back. At a signal all start chewing. They continue to chew until someone gets his piece of candy in his mouth. He is declared the winner. It is an exciting game to watch and equally funny to the players who have trouble to keep from laughing as they furiously chew.

Thanksgiving

TURKEY QUIZ

Furnish the players with paper and pencil. Read the following questionnaire. Be sure to allow enough time for each guest to write the answer to the questions as you read.

Answers

1. Name the part of the turkey that assists a lady in dressing.   Comb

2. Name the part of the turkey that opens the front door.   Key (last part)

3. Part of a turkey that appears after Thanksgiving.   Bill

4. Part of a turkey that's part of a sentence.   Claws (clause)

5. Part of a turkey that is used for cleaning.   Wings (dusters)

6. Part of a turkey that a farmer watches carefully.   Crop

7. Part of a turkey that is an oriental.   Turk (first part)

8. Why ought the turkey be ashamed?	We see the turkey dressing
9. Why is a fast eater like a turkey?	Both are fast gobblers
10. What color gets its name from turkey?	Turkey red
11. When the turkey is cooking what country is he in?	Grease (Greece)
12. What part of a turkey is a story?	Tail (tale)
13. What part of a turkey appears on the battlefield?	Drumstick

At the end of ten minutes read the correct answers. The individual with the greatest number of correct answers can be awarded a blue ribbon turkey cut from brown construction paper with a blue ribbon around its neck.

PIE TIN RELAY

Divide the group into two teams. Give each team leader a pie tin and an apple. At a signal the leader puts the pie tin with the apple in it on his head, runs a set distance, returns, and gives the tin and apple to the second in line. The first team to finish wins, and the members of the winning team can be given candy corn.

THANKSGIVING DAY SPEECH

Pick the most vocal to give a Thanksgiving day speech with plenty of gestures. Ask him to include in it the names of all barnyard animals. Tell each guest to keep an animal in mind. When the speaker raises his right hand, everyone immediately imitates the animal he has chosen. When he raises his left hand all keep silent. When he raises both hands everyone imitates a turkey's "gobble, gobble." All calls are continued until the speaker lowers his arms.

THANKSGIVING QUESTIONS

This Question and Answer game can be played either orally or with paper and pencil. If written, of course, paper and pencils must be furnished. For young children a suitable and not too hard list is:

	Answers
1. What is the Thanksgiving fowl?	Turkey
2. Who were the guests at the first Thanksgiving dinner?	Indians
3. Who were the hosts at the first American Thanksgiving dinner?	Puritans
4. Name one grain the Pilgrims found in the new world.	Corn
5. At what time of the year did the Pilgrims hold their first Thanksgiving?	In the Fall after Harvest

CRANBERRY RELAY RACE

Divide the crowd into two groups. Give the leader of each group four cranberries to put on the back of his hand. He must carry the four cranberries across the room and back and give them to the next in line. If one of the cranberries drops off, the player must stop and replace it before continuing the race. The line finishing first is the winner.

NUT-PITCHING CONTEST

An indoor nut pitching contest is good Thanksgiving day fun. For this game put a small bowl in a little larger bowl and place both in the center of a dishpan. Each player then takes a turn trying to throw three walnuts or peanuts into the smallest bowl. Score five points for the nuts landing in the center bowl, three points for the larger bowl, and one point for the dishpan. Let each contestant keep his own score. The player with the highest score may be given permission to wash and put away the two bowls and dishpan.

COUNT YOUR BLESSINGS

For this Thanksgiving game all players are seated in a circle. One player starts off with "I am grateful for apples" or something beginning with the letter "A." The next player is grateful for something beginning with "B" as "I am grateful for my brother." The third, "C," might say, "I am grateful for children to play with." So on around the circle and through the alphabet. If a player fails to think of a word beginning with the proper letter, he drops out of the circle. The one remaining in the circle longest can be given a chocolate turkey as a prize.

INDIAN TRADER

Players are divided into two groups and located at opposite ends of the room. One group is called "Traders" and the other "Indians." The traders decide among themselves upon some vegetable to sell to the Indians. When they have chosen one they march across the room and stand before the Indians. A spokesman says, "We have a vegetable to sell. Guess what." As soon as some Indians guess the right vegetable all the traders scoot for their own side of the room with the Indians in hot pursuit. If an Indian catches one of the traders, he must join the Indians. Then the Indians take their turn at selling vegetables.

Christmas

MEXICAN PINATE

In Mexico, instead of a Christmas tree, families have a pinate, which is a big paper-like bag hung from the ceiling. All presents for the family are put into this bag. On Christmas each child is blindfolded and given a long stick with which to break the pinate. If the bag is poked just right, it breaks quite easily, and all the presents spill on the floor. Everyone scrambles for the gift marked with his name.

CHRISTMAS QUIZ

Give the guests pencils and paper and ask them to answer the questions you read with titles of Christmas songs.

Questions	Answers
1. Why are the kids excited?	Santa Claus is Coming to Town
2. Give the exact name of an animal with a W. C. Fields proboscis.	Rudolf
3. Let's hitch up the horses and go on one	Sleighride
4. A decorator's holiday order	Deck the Halls
5. A wish for Christmas weather	Let It Snow
6. These are always an important part of song No. 3	Jingle Bells
7. A country known only to children	Toyland
8. What are you dreaming of at this time of year?	White Christmas
9. Describe Switzerland at Christmas time	Winter Wonderland
10. What would you like to read in a telegram delivered on Dec. 24th from a loved one far away?	I'll Be Home for Christmas

At the conclusion of the ten questions, read the correct answers. For those with all correct answers give a score of 100 for they are right in tune with Christmas. For six right out of ten give a score of 60 for they are still in key. For four right, give a score of 40 for those players are slightly off pitch. For two right, the player is flat and rates only a score of 20.

CROOKED QUESTIONS

Chairs, numbering one less than the number of players, are arranged in two rows facing each other. A space of a couple of yards should, if possible, be left between them. Someone is appointed Leader and may carry a bit of holly as an insignia of office. The Leader, passing back and forth between the chairs, asks questions on any subject which occurs to him. The queries should be in rapid succession and as he asks each, the Leader points with the holly to the person addressed.

According to the rules of the game, the person addressed must never answer. The reply must come from the player seated just opposite. The object of the Leader is either to obtain an answer from the person addressed or to catch the person seated opposite "napping." For those who fail the test, the Leader enacts a penalty. For example, the person failing may be condemned to draw the picture of Santa Claus in the air with his forefinger or to spell the word "Christmas" backwards.

CHRISTMAS

Give the guests pencils and paper. Let each one try to see how many words can be made from the word "Christmas." The one with the longest list of words wins the game.

CHRISTMAS BELLS

Suspend a large Christmas wreath in a doorway at a convenient height from the floor with a bell hidden in it. Prepare in advance "snowballs" made of cotton batting covered with white tissue paper.

The players stand about eight feet from the wreath. Each is given three "snowballs" and the one who succeeds in throwing all three, one at a time, through the wreath is given a prize.

To make it more exciting, sides may be chosen, and each one of the three snowballs numbered, one numbered 5, the second 10, and the third 20. If the ball numbered 5 goes through, it counts 5 for that player's side. If it does not go through, it is a loss. If the player hits the little bell, hidden in the wreath, it counts 25 for his side. The side scoring the most points is victorious.

CHRISTMAS CLIPPING MATCH

Stretch a cord across an open doorway and to it attach six or eight little net stockings filled with candy. At Christmas time these candy stockings are obtainable in all the candy stores. Each player is blindfolded and sent with scissors to clip down one of the stockings. The successful player keeps the stocking he captures.

PULL IN, PULL OUT

Draw a holly wreath on the floor in colored chalk, or if your amusement room is carpeted, cut a holly wreath from Christmas paper and pin it to the rug. Guests join hands and form a circle. To the accompaniment of quick music they dance about the wreath. As they dance they try to make some player touch the holly wreath. Anyone touching the wreath is debarred. Game continues until only one player remains. A small holly box filled with Christmas candy is an appropriate prize.

BONBON EXCHANGE

Game requires as many hard candies as there are guests. Wrap all the candies except one in silver paper.

Wrap the one in gilt paper. Place all the candy in a bag. Each guest shuts his eyes, puts his hand in and takes out a candy, taking care that no one else sees it. It is the aim of each player to get and retain the gold candy, for he who holds it when the bell rings twenty minutes later will receive a prize. If any player can guess in which hand another player is holding his bonbon, the player of whom the demand is made is obliged to open his hand and if it contains the gold bonbon, to give it up. The same two players cannot exchange again for five minutes, so it is impossible to win back the gold bonbon once it is lost without some measure of doubt and uncertainty.

CHRISTMAS CANDLES

Put a circle of small candles around a bouquet of holly on a table. Blindfold the player, turn him around three times, and allow him to take five steps toward the table. Then he must blow as hard as he can, trying to blow out all the candles at once. The player who succeeds in extinguishing the greatest number receives a prize.

SNAP DRAGON

A number of raisins are placed in a dish and alcohol or vanilla poured over them and set on fire. The object is to draw them out one by one.

CANDY TOSS

Guests are divided into couples. One of each couple stands in a line facing his partner in the opposite line. The two lines stand about eight feet apart.

Each player on one side has a dish of twenty-five pieces of hard candy individually wrapped. His partner opposite has a good-sized paper bag. When the music starts each one tries to throw as many pieces of candy as possible into his partner's bag. When the music stops, throwing stops. Candies thrown after the music ceases don't count. Music starts and stops several times before the last stop. At the end of the game the couple with the most candies in the bag wins.

14.

Games For The Very Young

Young children love to play games. Most parents miss a wonderful opportunity to have fun with their children because they overlook the fun of playing games with them. The games need not be difficult. Younger children like to play old favorites and the same game over and over. Group games should not be overlooked either. If well directed, group games encourage self-reliance, teach a sense of fair play and give a bit of social training. A party for young children should include active and inactive games, mixed with things to do. Here are some favorites for the very young.

GRUNT, PIGGY, GRUNT

One child is chosen "It" and must be blindfolded. The rest of the players take hands and form a circle around him. They walk around "It" clockwise, until he says "Stop." Then stretching out his arm he points to one player and says, "Grunt, piggy, grunt." The one to whom he points must imitate a pig, and "It" must try to guess who grunted. If he guesses correctly, the one who grunted must be "It" and take his place in the circle.

LITTLE TOMMY TITTLEMOUSE

Little Tommy Tittlemouse is tops with most children. One child hides behind a big chair where he can't be seen. A second child stands in front of the chair while the group sings:

"Little Tommy Tittlemouse sat in a little house,
Someone's knocking, Oh me, Oh my,
        (The child in front knocks on the chair)
Someone's calling—
        (The child knocking says, "It is I.")

The youngster in hiding must recognize the caller by his voice. It is amazing how quickly little children catch on to the various voices and recognize them.

STORY ACTING

Small youngsters adore a story in which they can participate. Pick a simple story like "William and His Kitten" by Marjorie Flack (Houghton). Assign to each child one of the characters of the story. For instance, let Tommy be the kitten and every time the kitten is mentioned in the story, Tommy mews. One child may be the postman, another the grocer, etc. When the postman is mentioned he whistles, the grocer says "Humph." With a bit of ingenuity you can find something for each child to do. When you read the story slow up a bit as you come to the characters, thus giving each child time to realize his turn has come. Even the most active child will listen to the story if he has a part in it.

PONY TROT

This circle game includes a chant which the leader can teach the children as they play the game. While chanting the first verse the children prance without going forward.

> "Trot, trot, trot, little pony trot
> Down the road so rough and stony,
> Trot along my little pony.
> Trot, trot, trot, trot, trot, little pony trot.

During the second verse all ponies run around the circle.

> "Run, run, run, little pony, run!
> Run along and do not stumble,
> Or I fear we both shall tumble.
> Run, run, run, run, run, little pony, run!

During the last verse the ponies all run to their stalls (chairs).

> "Rest, rest, rest, you have done your best.
> To the stable I will lead you,
> And on hay and oats I'll feed you,
> Rest, rest, rest, rest, rest, little pony, rest!

CAT AND CANARY

Players, all but two, form a circle holding hands to form a bird cage. One player becomes a canary and stands inside the cage and the other a cat and waits outside. All of a sudden the canary decides to fly out of the cage. He may go out between any two players in the circle and they must hold up their arms to let him through. Once he's outside the circle the cat starts to chase him and he must run completely around the circle once and go back between the same two players. The cat gets five points if he tags the canary. Otherwise the canary scores five points. As soon as either the cat or canary gain twenty points, a new cat and canary are chosen.

HOT BALL

All children sit in a circle. A good-sized ball, such as a basketball, is placed in center. The leader explains the ball is very hot and each child on receiving the ball must push it away as fast as possible. The leader then rolls the ball swiftly to a child, who quickly pushes it across the circle. The child to whom it rolls gives it a quick shove to another. This game is exciting for small children and teaches coordination.

HUNT THE SLIPPER

The children sit in a circle and all sing:

"Cobbler, cobbler, mend my shoe
Have it done by half past two
Stitch it up and stitch it down
Now see with whom the shoe is found."

A child in the center of the circle gives a shoe to a child, saying, "This must be mended quickly." The cobbler-child promises. The first child sits down to wait for his shoe. He closes his eyes. The shoe is passed from child to child as the song is chanted. As the last measure of music is sung the child holding the shoe puts it quickly behind him and resumes a natural position. The customer in the center demands his shoe. He must guess who has the shoe. Each child questioned answers "Yes" or "No." He has three turns to guess where the shoe is. Then another child becomes the customer.

RING BELL RING

One child closes his eyes while another child is given a little bell to hold by the clapper while he runs to hide in some distant part of the room or next room. The first child calls "Ring, bell, ring." The second child rings the bell and the first child points in the direction of the sound. If he points in the right direction, he then becomes the bell ringer. If he does not point in the right direction, the second child remains the bell ringer.

POLICEMAN AND LOST CHILD

This is best played with a group of children. One child is a Policeman and "Mother" worriedly asks his help in searching for her lost child. The policeman asks Mother to tell him what her lost child is wearing. The mother describes in detail the clothes which her lost child has on. The Policeman looks about the children and brings to Mother the child answering the description. For a large group several children can be "lost," with one child acting as Mother and another as Policeman.

WHEELBARROW RACE

Players form in double line. First-line players place their hands on the floor on count one; on count two, second-line players grasp the ankles of the player in front and lift the feet; and on three, the first-line player walks on his hands to the goal line and returns. Those holding the handles of the wheelbarrow (ankles of first players) may not push, but let the wheelbarrow set his own pace, or he will fall on his nose and the race will be lost. The wheelbarrow returning first with no mishaps wins the race.

FINGER PAINTING

Little children love to paint with their fingers. All that is necessary are sheets of clean white paper—smooth wrapping paper will do—and a supply of finger paint. Finger painting for little folks is best if confined to one color on a sheet of clean white paper.

With his fingers the child smears the paint all over the paper. Then while it's still wet he makes a design, using only his fingers. When the sheet is dried you'll be surprised at the lovely picture he has created.

Finger paint can be purchased, but it also can be made very inexpensively at home. Dissolve one-eighth cup of laundry starch in a half cup of cold water. Add to a pint of boiling water and cook about five minutes, stirring constantly to keep the mixture smooth. Add vegetable coloring and let cool. Your finger paint is ready to use.

LOCOMOTIVE

Children scatter about in couples. One member of each couple stands behind the other and puts his arms around his partner. This forms the engine and caboose. One who is "It" tries to catch a ride by putting his arms around the "caboose" (the one behind). If he succeeds, the engine (the one in front) must leave his place and be "It."

CROSSING THE BROOK

Mark two lines about two feet apart on the floor. White bias tape pinned at each end to the carpet make good lines. These lines represent the banks of a brook. The children then try to jump the brook without getting wet feet. When they have succeeded in jumping the brook, one bank is moved farther away and they try jumping this wider brook, always with the idea in mind that if they don't reach the other shore, they'll have wet feet.

MOTHER KITTY

The leader tells a story saying that Mother Kitty and Baby Kitty are fast asleep. The Baby Kitty wakes up and runs away to hide while Mother Kitty sleeps on. When Mother Kitty awakens to find the Baby

Kitty gone, Mother calls "Meow." The Baby Kitty answers "Mew." The youngsters like to dramatize this story as it is told. There may be any number of baby kitties. Of course, the game is to have Mother Kitty locate her babies by sound. She may call "Meow" until she locates their "Mews."

TOUCH

This simple game pleases young children. It consists of identifying objects in a cloth bag. Put three to six objects that are familiar to a child such as a ball, pencil, toy boat, automobile or airplane, and animals of various kinds into a cloth bag. Let the child identify them by feeling in the bag.

BECKONING GAME

For variation from noisy games, little children find tremendous fascination about a "Choosing game" that proceeds entirely in silence. The children stand in a circle, one child in the center. He beckons to a child in the circle. That child comes into the circle and shakes hands with the first child. The first child goes out into the circle and the second child repeats the action of the first child. The game continues in silence until each child has been beckoned to.

RING MASTER

The children form a circle and one child acts as Ring Master in the center. The Ring Master walks around waving his wand and calling the name of some animal. The children in the circle immediately imitate that animal, dancing like bears, waddling like ducks, galloping like horses and growling, quacking or whinnying as the case may be. Then the Ring Master calls, "The circus parade will begin;" each child chooses an animal he wishes to imitate and moves around the circle with movements characteristic of his choice.

MRS. BROWN'S PARTY

A child starts the story, "Mrs. Brown had at her party . . ." then he walks around the room touching one object. The next child says, "Mrs. Brown had at her party . . ." and then he touches the first object touched and adds one of his own. This can be continued with first one child and then the other until eight or ten objects have been touched before the game ends.

FIVE LITTLE CHICKADEES

This musical game is a favorite with young children. It is accompanied by a simple tune: Five children sit in a doorway. As each verse is sung the chickadees in turn fly from the group about the room and settle in the opposite corner of the room. When the song is finished they are all bunched in the opposite corner ready "to do it again."

1. "Five little chickadees sitting in the door
   One flew away and then there were four.
2. Four little chickadees sitting in a tree
   One flew away and then there were three.
3. Three little chickadees looking at you
   One flew away and then there were two.
4. Two little chickadees having lots of fun
   One flew away and then there was one.
5. One little chickadee left all alone
   He flew away and then there were none."

SKIP TAG

The children stand in a circle with one hand outstretched, palm up. One child skips inside circle to music (any good skipping music) and touches a second child's hand. Second child skips in opposite direction. The two meet, grasp right hands and dance around each other. The first child goes to his place and the second child proceeds as did the first.

Variation: Some young children do not skip easily. For them substitute marching music and make it a Walking Tag.

ELF GARDEN

An elf garden will bring endless delight to any youngster. Get a flat box, such as is used in greenhouses to start plants. Line the box with heavy tar paper to keep the wet earth from soaking through. Put in a layer of rich ground. Place a small mirror— one from an old purse will do nicely—for a lake. Then let your child help you lay out the garden. Evergreen twigs make excellent trees, and slips from colored foliage plants make colorful borders. Grass, planted in the open areas, if well watered, will sprout in three days. A sand walk with pebble borders will add to the view. Such a garden will delight any child, and its possibilities for development are endless.

BUCKET BALL

While most children can't catch a ball until they are four or over, nevertheless games with a ball delight them. One such game is "Bucket Ball." Place a waste-basket in the center of the room and then the young-sters try to throw a tennis ball into the basket. The children take turns, or the child to whom the ball rolls may throw. As the child develops his skill he can try bouncing the ball into the basket. If the ball goes into the basket, he gets another turn.

ROCK HUNT

The very young enjoy hunting for tiny pebbles or pretty stones, especially if they have a rock box made for the occasion. Cut the top from a two quart milk carton. Make a sturdy handle of string and the rock box is ready to be filled. Small youngsters will keep busy for hours filling their "rock box" with treasures.

BLOWING BUBBLES

Nothing is more fun than blowing bubbles. This requires an old-fashioned clay pipe, two-thirds of a quart of soapy water, a teaspoonful of sugar and four tablespoonfuls of glycerine or vegetable oil for dura-ble bubbles. From this you can blow bubbles that will hop and dance through the air.

PUSS IN A CORNER

All players except one, the Pussy, are stationed in corners or at convenient goals which will serve the purpose. On the playground trees make good goals. The odd player goes from one player to another say-ing, "Pussy wants a corner." While the attention of

Puss is attracted to some other player, two players should try to exchange places. Puss tries to steal a corner while this exchange takes place. If she succeeds, the player left without a home becomes Puss; if Puss does not succeed in getting a corner after several attempts, she may call "All change," when all must hurry to new corners or goals, while Puss finds one for herself. The odd player becomes the new Puss.

KNOW ME?

One child is asked to close his eyes or is blindfolded. The leader or teacher beckons to a child in the group. He goes up and shakes hands with the child. The blindfolded child then tries to identify his caller by feeling of his head and his clothes.

PAPER CHAINS

All youngsters love to make decorative paper chains. Use two colors of crepe paper—whatever colors are appropriate to the occasion. For instance, black and orange are ideal for Halloween. Cut two strips of crepe paper, one black and one orange, of equal length and equal width. Two inches is a good width. Fasten with a common pin, or paste the strips together at right angles to each other. Then fold the orange strip over the black, then the black over the orange. Continue until the entire lengths are folded. You will now have a pile of folded squares. Stick or pin the end together. Then pull out the folded papers. You will have a very attractive black and orange chain.

15.

Teen-Age Games

Many teen-agers scorn games as "kid stuff" and rightly so when they are asked to play "Pin the Tail on the Donkey," or "Drop clothespins into a milk bottle." However, they do enjoy games that call for partners, and offer some opportunity for skill and imagination.

VIVID IMAGINATION

This game is played by couples sitting in chairs which are placed back to back. The man is given a pencil, sheet of paper and something stiff to use as a drawing board. The girl is given an object. She must not tell her partner what it is, nor must she let him see it. She describes it to him in terms of shape, size, lines, etc. (The object can be a pair of scissors, a hat, pitcher, or almost anything.) Her partner then draws a picture, following her directions. When everyone has finished, the pictures and objects should be displayed—side by side. The winning picture is the one most closely resembling the original object.

THE SURPRISE PACKAGE

Divide the crowd into groups of four or five. Each group is given a pair of dice, a dinner plate with a package in the middle and a knife and fork laid on top of the package.

The package consists of a small, plain Hershey bar wrapped in a newspaper, and tied criss-cross with string. This is then wrapped in another newspaper and again tied with many strings.

The first player to roll a pair with the dice takes the knife and fork and tries to unwrap the package. He may use only the knife and fork.

While he works with the package, the other players take turns rolling the dice. The first one to succeed in rolling a pair, takes the knife and fork from the first player and continues to unwrap the package. Each one works until another player rolls a pair.

If at any time the package falls off the plate while a contestant is trying to untie it, he loses his turn and the next successful dice roller gets it.

The player who finally gets the package open down to the chocolate bar proceeds to unwrap the bar and eat it with knife and fork, unless someone rolls a pair before he finishes.

CAR SCRAMBLE

For a group of "hot-rodders" or car enthusiasts try "Car Scramble." The challenger names some make of car. Next in line names a car beginning with the last letter of the first car named. For instance, if the challenger says "Buick," the next person may say "Kaiser." This is an interesting game because someone is sure to remember old makes of cars forgotten by almost everyone.

LOST LOVER

Players are seated in a circle with "It" blindfolded in the center. "It" gropes about in search of a seated player, then drops to his knees and says to the one seated, "Are you my lost lover?" The victim answers with a disguised voice. He or she may bark like a dog, meow like a cat, groan, or answer in any manner he wishes, as "It" tries to recognize who he or she is. One guess is allowed. If "It" guesses correctly, the victim takes "It's" place. If not, "It" tries again.

NOSE GAME WITH FUNNY FACES

For this game have a talented friend draw six funny faces about dinner plate size on a strip of brown paper about eight feet long. Cut the nose out of each face. Stretch up the brown paper. The girls stand behind the brown paper, sticking their noses through the opening on the faces. Each escort looks over the row of noses, decides which one belongs to his girl, then he proceeds to kiss the nose he thinks he brought.

HOW GREEN YOU ARE

"How Green You Are" is a hilarious game. One person leaves the room. While he is gone the group decides what he is to do when he is called back. It might be decided that he is to smell a flower on the table, take off his shoes, or stand on his head. As soon as he responds to the call, "ready," the group sings "How Green You Are" to the tune of "Auld Lang Syne" while he is trying to discover what is expected of him. When he gets nearer the object involved, or nearer to accomplishing the feat, the crowd sings louder. When he gets farther away the singing grows softer. It is amazing how complicated the stunts can be and still be accomplished.

CRAZY GIVERS

Ask each player to bring, wrapped as a dainty gift, the one thing in his possession for which he has no earthly use. It can be anything! When everyone has arrived, write the name of each guest on pieces of paper, fold them and shuffle them in a hat. Ask someone to draw two names at a time from the hat and read them aloud. The two persons whose names are called then exchange their gift packages. When all names have been drawn, open the gifts one at a time so everyone can enjoy the fun!

HUMAN TIC TAC TOE

Place three chairs in a row—three chairs directly behind each of the first three chairs to make a second row. Complete the square by putting three more chairs directly behind the first two rows. You now have a tic-tac-toe square made of nine chairs. The first girl player sits in any chair of her choice. A boy takes a chair of his choice, keeping in mind that he must sit so as to keep the girls from completing a row of three girls. The next girl tries to sit so as to continue the girls' line and block the boys. Boys and girls alternate taking seats until either the girls or boys complete an unbroken line of three, or, as is sometimes the case, all lines are blocked. Then the cat gets that game. This is a popular game with teen-agers.

SPOONING

The leader chooses three couples to do a bit of spooning. Partners are seated on opposite sides of the table and each is given a spoon. The spoons are tied together with about eight inches of string. Then each contestant is given a dish of ice cream. The object of the game is to see which couple can finish its ice cream without breaking the string. At a signal the race begins. A broken string disqualifies a couple. Winners are awarded wooden spoons.

SILHOUETTE

To pick partners hang a sheet in an open doorway between two rooms. Put the men in a darkened room. In the other room turn on bright lights directly back of the sheet. The women then walk between the light and sheet. Each man chooses his partner from the shadow on the sheet.

MALE DRESSMAKERS

Give each couple several newspapers and a supply of pins. Ask each man to make a dress for his partner. He chooses his own style of dress, tears the papers at will, and pins a dress of paper on his lady.

Of course the women are ready with plenty of suggestions. You'll be amazed at some of the newspaper creations these young male dressmakers turn out. A prize can be given for the most attractive, the most unusual or the most skillful.

16.

Creative Play

The creative urge is strong in all of us. And sometimes this urge can be diverted into a party activity, such as finger painting for tiny folks, flower making for young girls, carpenter efforts for boys.

Some games call for equipment that can be made at home such as bean bag board, and rollerskate polo. These homemade games are welcome for home recreation and for use in informal gatherings. The partnership value of games is important, whether the game is played by two or three, or by a big group.

SNOWFLAKES

Small youngsters always love to make snowflakes and sometimes older youngsters find it fun. Fold a square of tissue paper into halves, then into quarters, and then into eighths. Snip off here and there a corner of the folded tissue. When unfolded the result will be an intricate snowflake pattern.

PUPPET HEADS

Equipment: a cardboard tube large enough for a finger to enter — newspaper, facial tissue, string, rope, yarn, beads or buttons.

Crumple a newspaper into an egg shape about three inches in diameter. Stick ends of newspaper into three-inch cardboard tube which forms the neck of a puppet. Fasten to the tube with string.

Soak several facial tissues in liquid starch and model on egg-shape foundation. (Very soft toilet paper will do as well.) Make the nose and features of the puppet by building up layers of wet paper. Allow to dry. Cover the rest of the egg-shape with three-inch squares of tissue soaked in starch. Then give the entire head surface a final coating of starch-dipped paper to insure a smooth, hard finish.

When dry, paint the entire head with flesh-toned paint. Allow to dry once more. Mix water colors with starch and paint in desired features.

Frayed rope fastened with glue can be used for hair. Beads, thumbtacks or buttons can be eyes.

LOG CABIN

Equipment: liquid starch, sawdust, and a cardboard box.

Use one and one-third cups of sawdust to each cup of liquid starch or until the mixture feels right for modeling. This mixture can be put on any base, such as a cardboard box house.

Cut and shape a cabin from a cardboard box. Put on the starch mixture and let dry. Groove the mixture to represent logs. The result will be natural wood-color log cabin, which the youngsters can paint if they wish.

CARNATIONS

Equipment: colored toilet paper of the double thickness variety—wire for stems, plastic calyxes, paper carnation leaves and a roll of green tape to wrap the stems.

Tear off three pieces of toilet tissue two sheets long. Lay them flat one on top of the other. (Counting the double sheets as two you will now have six thicknesses of paper.) Starting at one end, accordion pleat the paper. Pinch it together firmly in the center and fasten it securely with one end of the stem wire. While the paper is still in folds, round off each end and cut tiny slashes across the scallops to give the ragged effect of carnation petals. Then gently separate each sheet of paper.

Slip a plastic calyx onto the wire stem up next to the flower head. Then wrap the stem with the green tape. About two inches down the wire stem wrap in two paper leaves. Add a second pair further down the stem. Draw the leaf over the dull side of a pairing knife until it curls like a carnation leaf.

Lovely bouquets can be made from the various colored carnations.

HATS

For this game provide each player with a hard-boiled egg, or one of the large plastic ones now used to trick unsuspecting hens. Also give each one a supply of bits of ribbon, felt, straw, sequins, lace, and cardboard. Suggest to the contestants that they can make a paper collar from the cardboard which will hold the egg upright. At a given signal each contestant proceeds to put a face on the egg and design a hat to fit the egg's personality.

Plenty of time should be allowed for this creative activity. A prize may be awarded to the "most stylish," the "fanciest," the "funniest," and the "most lifelike."

Variation: Large English walnuts may replace the eggs as models.

TABLE ORNAMENT

Equipment: a wooden bowl, supply of tiny straw flowers in red and yellow, bunch of transparent floral tape, small sack of patching plaster, box of small stones, a short gnarled tree branch.

The first step is to mix plaster to the consistency of soft butter in the wooden bowl. Into this mixture stick the short, gnarled branch. Over the plaster lay a cover of attractive stones. Before taking the next step let the plaster dry so the branch will be firmly held.

When the plaster is hardened, fasten tiny straw flowers onto the branch by wrapping transparent floral tape around it. The resulting centerpiece is comparable to the expensive ones found in stores.

BALLOON PUPPETS

Did you ever make a balloon puppet? They are lots of fun and you are limited only by your imagination. First inflate an ordinary balloon. Tie it as close up as possible, leaving the neck of the balloon free. Because rubber is slick, first rub the balloon with soapy lather. This soapy covering when dry makes the paint adhere more easily to the rubber.

The next step is to paint faces on the balloons. Either tempera paint or ink can be used.

When the features are completed to your satisfaction, dress up your balloon. Design a hat from crepe paper and stick it on with cellulose tape, or tie it on with ribbons under the chin. A Chinaman's queue can be made of braided black embroidery cotton.

To make your puppet stand alone slip the neck of the balloon through a slit in the center of a good-sized piece of stiff cardboard. If he's lonesome, try making him a girl friend with another balloon. Your balloon puppets will last for days and be jolly good friends.

FINGER FAIRIES

Have you ever seen a "Finger Fairy"? Draw or trace on heavy white paper a figure such as Santa Claus, a clown, or a doll—do not draw the legs. In the lower part of the body make two round holes. Slide your first two fingers through these holes to serve as legs. Your "Finger Fairy" will walk or dance. He'll be as lively as your fingers.

PAPIER MACHE ANIMALS

Making papier-mache animals is a sit-at-table activity that requires only three basic steps and a lot of patience.

First roll up newspapers to form the basic parts of the animal you have chosen. These parts are then tied together in the general shape of such animal—giraffe, horse, or whatever you want your animal to be.

Next the form is covered and filled in with strips of newspaper dipped in or covered with a flour-and-water mixture (about the consistency of cream).

This is allowed to harden. Then the animal is painted with bright poster paint colors, either realistically or imaginatively. When the paint is dry, a coat of shellac may be added to preserve the work.

COFFEE CUP CLOWNS

Equipment: paper coffee cup with handle, cone - shaped paper cup and paper baking cup, paste, crayons, and scissors.

Draw a face on the coffee cup with an extra handle added for the second ear. Decorate the cone-shaped paper cup with many colored dots for the hat and paste onto the coffee cup. The pleated paper baking cup makes the ruff. Children love to create these clowns. By sticking a hand in the paper cup, the clown can be made to turn its head, bow and do other clownish maneuvers.

DARTS

For children old enough to play with sharp-pointed darts, here's a homemade game that's fun. Make three darts by cutting the heads from matches. Slit one end so that a piece of folded paper about two and one-half inches square can be slipped into the slit. Into the other end of the match force the eye-end of a large sewing needle.

A circular target whose outside circle is not more than fifteen inches in diameter can be drawn on a wallboard or a piece of heavy cardboard and hung shoulder high on the wall.

The players stand about eight feet away from the target and each tries to throw the three darts so as to pierce the target as near the bull's-eye as possible. For each dart that sticks firmly in a space the player receives the number of points marked in that space. Nothing is counted for darts touching a line.

BEAN BAG BOARD

A clever bean-bag board can be made from a board about two feet wide and two and one-half or three feet long. Holes must be cut in it for eyes, nose and mouth. The openings for the eyes should be about seven inches long and five inches wide. The mouth should be about four inches long and ten inches wide. The base of the nose triangle should be about eight inches long. This board can be placed either against the wall or supported by a hinged prop.

BEAN BAGS

Players stand in line ten to fifteen feet from the bean bag board. Each player has five bean bags, or five bags may be used by several players in turn. A bag thrown into the mouth counts five points, one into the nose ten points, and for each eye twenty points. The first player to get one hundred points is winner.

WINDMILLS

All children love windmills and they are easily made. Take a piece of colored construction paper about four inches square and cut or tear from each corner to within three-fourths of an inch of the center. Pick up on the end of a pin—piercing from the back to the front—four alternate half corners. After you have the four half corners on the pin, put the point through the exact center of the paper and mount the wheel on the end of a stick or against some flat surface where the wind will make it whirl. The eraser end of a pencil is a good spot on which to stick your windmill.

To add variety to the windmill making, let the child use white paper and color designs on the square before it is pinned into shape.

SPOOL ANIMALS

Youngsters like to create spool animals. All that is needed are some empty spools, cardboard, glue, and crayons. For instance, for a spool dog, cut a dog's head out of cardboard tapering into a long neck which fits into one end of the spool. The face can be drawn with black crayon. Cut a long curved tail from the cardboard and insert it into the other end of the spool. It will look as if it would wag any minute. Cut four cardboard legs and glue them to the sides of the spool. It will make a surprisingly good-looking dog. Almost every kind of spool animal can be made by young fingers if their owners have good imaginations.

SPOOL WIND-UP CARS

Equipment: large spool, button (underwear size), rubber band, some match sticks, cellulose tape.

Thread the rubber band through one hole in the button. It can be forced through with a pin if necessary. Then put a match, with the head removed, through the loop so that the rubber band won't slip out of the button. Put the other end of the rubber band through the spool and hold it there by a short piece of match stick. To keep this end from slipping, tape it to the end of the spool.

The car is now all ready to be wound up. The button serves as a bearing. Twist the crank or long match stick until the rubber band is tight and put the spool on the floor. The little spool car will run rapidly across the room. These are tops in fun and much more exciting for children than any commercial wind-up car.

JAR RING TOSS

For this game prepare a board about twenty-eight inches square by driving at an angle twenty-three nails three inches long part way into it, or by screwing into it little right-angle hooks like those used to hold curtain rods. Each hook is given a value of 25, 20, 15, 10, or 5 points. Figures can be cut from a calendar and pasted on.

The board can be hung against the wall or set on a table. Its center should be about shoulder high. The players stand ten feet from the board. Each is given twelve rubber jar rings, which he tries to throw onto the nails or hooks having the highest numbers. The players throw three times in a play and rotate four times. It is well to mark the rings with crayon or paint so that each person may identify his own in counting the final score.

MISS THE BELL

This game is fun and easy to arrange. A bell is suspended in a hoop about eight inches in diameter and a small ball is given to the players. They take turns tossing the ball through the hoop without causing the bell to ring. One point is scored each time the ball goes through and three points are scored if the bell does not ring.

BALLOON TRICK

Do you know how to fasten toy balloons to walls or ceiling? It can be easily done without paste and without leaving a mark. It is fun to do and is quite mystifying. Also it makes pretty and unusual decorations for festive occasions.

Inflate the balloons to full capacity. Hold the balloon firmly in both hands and rub one side of the balloon briskly on a wool rug. Touch the rubbed spot quickly to the wall or ceiling and take your hands away. The balloon will stick for several days. The friction acts as paste. As the balloons become deflated they drop to the floor.

POTATO PRINTING

Equipment: potato, tempera paint, a newspaper to work on, paring knife.

Cut about one and one-half inches off one end of a raw potato. Trace on the cut end of the potato the design you wish to make. Then cut away the background about one-half inch deep around the design.

Wipe all moisture from the design and you are ready to paint it. Use the paint sparingly to avoid smearing. When the paint is dry you have a design to stamp on a white card, paper, or cloth.

KITE BUILDING

A kite is really simple to make. The frame is made with two sticks to form a cross, or three sticks to form an "X" with a cross piece. Tiny nails must be used to nail the sticks in the form wished.

By cutting a groove in the ends of the sticks, a strong string can be strung from stick to stick forming the frame on which to stick the paper.

The kite frame may then be covered with common tissue paper, lightweight wrapping paper, or even newspaper. Crepe paper is very decorative but it is a little harder to paste, but kites covered with crepe paper fly smoothly.

The tail of the kite must be as light as possible to avoid weighing down the kite. Tie small pieces of paper about a foot apart on a long light string. The small pieces of paper are loosely rolled, then tied in the middle like a bow.

SAFETY RULES FOR GOOD KITE FLYING

Rules issued by the Safety Service of Electrical Companies and the National Safety Company:

A good kite flier does not fly his kite near electric, telephone, or trolley wires, or near high voltage transmission towers.

He does not use wire or tinsel twine of any sort or even wet string.

He does not fly his kite in a thunderstorm.

He does not use a kite with metal ribs.

He does not run across highways but flies his kite in open places away from traffic.

ROLLER SKATE POLO

This fast and furious roller skate game can be played in the basement. Each player wields a croquet mallet but only one ball is used. A goal is set up at each end of the basement and the game is on. The players choose sides and each team tries to get the ball into the opponent's goal. The team first making five goals is the winner.

OBSTACLE COURSE

Another original roller skate game suitable to be played in the basement is "Obstacle Course." Tin cans salvaged from the rubbish box are set up at various distances and skaters maneuver through the openings between cans much as a skier maneuvers around trees on an open hillside. The one who is able to skate through the obstacle course in the shortest time wins.

BARREL TOSS

Players stand about twenty feet away from a barrel and throw stones or wooden blocks into it. Each may have five throws and a point may be awarded for each stone or block that goes in. The throwing line may be put farther back when the players are experts.

ENLARGING PICTURES

Have you ever wished you could paint large suitable pictures on your amusement room walls or a picture just right for your own room? You can do it easily even though you are not an artist.

Here is a simple practical way. Pick out from a magazine a picture you admire. Today's magazines have many attractive picture advertisements worth copying.

For instance, if you want to decorate your amusement room walls with pictures of dogs, find a dog picture that appeals to you. Suppose you want a picture three times the size of the original. Mark off one-inch squares on the small picture. This process is called "squaring it up."

Then on a large sheet of light brown paper (or on the back of old wallpaper) mark off an equal number of three-inch squares. This means that the large sheet of paper will have exactly the same number of squares as the small picture except that they will be much larger—in this case three times as large as the original picture.

The parts of the drawing which appear in each small square may readily be drawn in the corresponding squares of the large sheet. Begin at the upper left hand corner and copy in the large squares exactly the same outline that appears in the corresponding square on the small picture.

When the outline is completed, cut away from the big figure the surrounding paper. You will have a perfect pattern for the enlarged picture.

Fasten this large pattern to the basement wall with gummed tape and draw the outline on the wall. Remove the pattern and color the dog as it appeared in the original small picture.

Pastel chalk should be used for the work. It not only does beautiful work but it can be erased in case of errors.

To preserve the picture spray it with a plastic fixative. Care must be taken to spray the fixative as rubbing it on would smear the chalk. Fixatives can be bought at any hardware store, or you can make your own by mixing five parts of wood alcohol with one part of white shellac. Spray over the drawing and allow to dry for a few minutes. The shellac dulls delicate colors a trifle but it will not injure the picture.

FUNNY ANIMALS

Place a bowl of fruit, a dish of cloves, some black jelly beans, some pieces of yarn, a box of toothpicks, and a pincushion of pins on a table. Suggest that each one make a funny animal. To start the fun off you might suggest a pig with a lemon body—knob end for snout. Black-headed pins for eyes, a bit of curly yarn for a tail and toothpicks for legs. An interesting turtle can be made of a large flat raisin with cloves for the legs, tail and head. The variety of possibilities is endless and your crowd will soon be on its way with turkeys, chickens, dogs, and many other funny animals.

A METAL PLAQUE FOR YOUR ROOM

Modeling of sheet metal is a very ancient art. The early Egyptians made much use of it and museums have exhibits of it, including jewelry, ornaments and masks from other ancient peoples.

Metal has always been one of the most widely used construction materials for the craftsman and is popular today with the young modern who likes to try his skill.

Why not begin with thin metal modeling? There are many types of metals: copper, pewter, brass, aluminum and tin foil which can be worked into beautiful and attractive ornaments.

A metal plaque is easy to make. All the tools you need are a sheet of thin pliable metal, a piece of felt as large as the metal you are using, a piece of soft wood on which to work and some tooling instruments. You can buy regular tooling instruments or you can substitute a nut pick, an orange wood stick or a sharpened piece of wood for them.

Lay the felt on the wooden block. If you have no

felt, several folds of newspaper will do just as well. Place your sheet of metal on the felt. Choose a picture you want on your plaque. A simple one is better than one with too much detail. Center it on your metal and secure it with gummed tape. With the rounded side of a nut pick trace over the lines of the picture, pressing hard enough to make an indentation in the metal.

When the outline of the picture is clear-cut on the metal remove the picture and turn the metal face up. In order to make the picture outline on the metal stand out clearly press down on the background with dull rounded tool or fingernail orange wood stick.

By working first on one side, then on the other, your design will stand out in clear relief. If you are working with thin copper or any soft material, you should fill in the back of the raised portions with clay and let harden.

To antique the copper plaques brush them with a weak sulphuric acid solution (obtainable at any hobby craft shop) and let stand a few minutes. Then thoroughly wash the plaque to remove acid. Rub the entire surface with very fine steel wool (No. 000). This will burnish the raised portions of the plaque and leave the background with a darkened antique effect which adds to its beauty.

The finished plaque can be tacked onto a piece of wood and hung on the wall, or it can be framed like a picture.

TOOLS SUGGESTED FOR METAL TOOLING

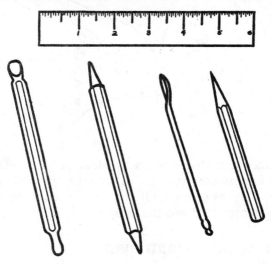

Any fine-grained hard wood, such as birch, maple, or lemon, may be used to make homemade tools in sketch.

FLYING BIRD

An attractive flying bird to be hung in the window or on the Christmas tree can be made from aluminum foil. Fold the foil through the center. Mark the outline of the bird on the folded aluminum foil, then with tin snips cut out the bird. By spreading out its wings and tail it will seem to be flying through the air. Sequins or little bright stones can be pasted onto the metal bird with a bit of household glue or enamel.

Place a dotted line on the fold of the metal and trace around the pattern. Cut out with tin snips. Apply detail lines as desired. Glue colored sequins in appropriate places to finish the design.

FLYING CARDBOARD BIRD

Cut the little six-inch body from cardboard. Color the body with crayon and paint a bright eye on both sides of the body. Then cut a slit through the body, near the shoulders, for the wings. A slit at the rear will allow the tail to be slipped into place and glued into position.

The colored wings can be made of colored construction paper or even tinted stationery, and folded in bellows fashion, back and forth, in one-inch folds. Slip wings through a wing slot. Cut the tail from the same kind of paper in a V-shape, and fold in one-fourth inch folds towards the point of the V. Glue the tail in position. Punch a hole in the back of the bird for a string. Attach the bird to the chandelier or in an open window or on the porch, and watch him fly.

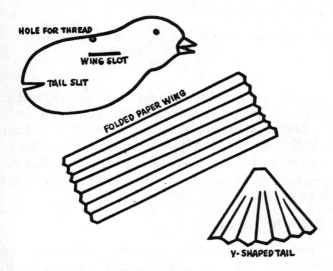

HOLE FOR THREAD

WING SLOT

TAIL SLIT

FOLDED PAPER WING

Y-SHAPED TAIL

FLYING CARDBOARD BIRD

SAND PAINTING

Equipment needed—Small supply of fine white sand
                   Piece of white paper
                   Tube of glue
                   Dye

To dye sand mix several pie tins of colored water. To color the water you can use crepe paper, vegetable dye; household bluing, iodine, or mercurochrome. Pour a small amount of sand into each color and then dry it.

Draw a design on the paper. Smear glue within the design. Then sift sand onto the glue according to the colors desired.

LEAF PICTURES

Put a maple or oak leaf on a sheet of construction paper. Anchor it with little stones. Dip an old toothbrush into tempera watercolor and spatter (by rubbing a thumb along the bristles) tiny dots of paint on the background. When the leaves and stones are removed you have a silhouette-type picture.

A simple frame for your picture can be made by finding four little twigs that are fairly straight. Lash the twigs together at the corners with yarn. Attach the picture to the frame with thumb tacks.

BUTTERFLY NET

Every youngster loves to catch butterflies. A very simple net can be easily made with a wire coat hanger bent into a circle—the hook part serving as the handle. A piece of cheesecloth sewed to the circle becomes the net.

17.

Be Your Own Weatherman

Is it going to snow? Will it be warmer? Will it rain the day of our picnic? People are always talking about the weather and no wonder because the weather and its variations are extremely interesting and very important in our lives. The fellow who is always predicting just what the weather will be is a nuisance but the real scientific weather forecaster is a very useful citizen.

Have you ever thought of setting up a little weather bureau and doing a little scientific forecasting on your own? You can have oodles of fun, get a lot of information and collect valuable data with a few simple instruments.

And the best of it is you can make practically all the instruments you need yourself—a weather vane, wind measurer, floral barometer, weather glass, and rain gauge.

WEATHER VANE

For the simplest weather vane all that is needed is a wooden arrow, a wire nail, and a pole on which to mount it. The wooden arrow should be at least two feet long and at least four inches wide. This can be whittled out of orange box crate wood or a shingle. Bore a hole through the exact center of the arrow so that it will turn easily on a wire nail with which it is fastened to a pole.

For a more complicated weather vane the arrow can be set in a large spool which has been notched to hold the arrow. A short piece of brass rod—like mother uses for her curtains—is inserted in the spool. The other end of the rod fits into the pole or post which supports the weather vane. A little grease smeared on the rod will prevent friction and help the vane to turn easily.

The tip of the arrow will always point to the direction from which the wind blows. A coat of paint or varnish will protect your weather vane from weathering and eliminate the danger of the wood cracking or warping.

So that you will always know which direction the wind is coming from it is well to mark your weather vane with the four points of the compass. The letters N S E and W for North, South, East and West can be made from sheet metal or tin.

If you have no tin handy, use a tin can. An ordinary size vegetable or fruit can will be big enough to give you metal to work with. Cut the bottom out of the can and then with tin snips cut open the can from top to bottom. This is done with the shears along one edge of the side seam. When handling tin shears to cut tin, be sure to hold them at right angles to the surface being cut. If the shears are held at a slanting angle to the surface, metal as thin as tin plate will buckle and the shears will not cut it.

You will now have a semi-round sheet of tin plate which must be flattened. This can be done in a number of ways. Because tin plate has a certain amount of "spring" in it, sometimes you can flatten it by bending it the other way. Or you can rub out the curve by rubbing the convex side of the curved sheet back and forth over the edge of a box or work bench. Or you can tap out the curve with a wooden mallet, working from one end of the plate slowly to the other across the width of the sheet.

You will now have smooth sheets of tin from which to cut your letters. Better make a paper pattern first. The letters should be about three inches high. Paste the paper patterns on the sheet metal as a guide and cut the letters out with the tin snips.

Fasten each letter on a wooden rod about thirteen inches long. The tin is soft and can be easily tacked onto it. This in turn can be tacked onto the pole under the weathervane. Use a compass to be sure that you are getting your directions exactly right. The weather vane is now finished and you can accurately observe the direction of the wind. You will want to jot it down each day in your daily weather report.

ANEMOMETER

Every amateur weatherman should have an anemometer—an instrument to measure the speed of the wind. At the weather station the anemometer consists of four cones which catch the wind and revolve at various speeds. A dial on the instrument records the number of revolutions of the cones and registers the exact speed of the wind.

Of course, the wind speeder that you can make will have no dial, but you can estimate the speed of the wind by noticing how fast the cones spin around.

There are several ways of making an anemometer but the simplest is by fastening four small funnels to the ends of two rods about two feet long. The two funnels at the ends of each rod should be facing in opposite directions. The holes in the funnels should be firmly plugged with corks. Nail the two rods at right angles to each other onto the top of a big spool. One end of a short piece of round brass rod is then inserted into the spool and the other end into the pole on which your anemometer is erected. Be sure this rod is well greased so that your wind-speeder will revolve easily.

Paint the tin cones and rods so as to protect them from the weather. Paint three of the cones or funnels a light color and the fourth one a dark color so that it will be easily distinguished as it whirls around. By watching the dark cone as it spins and timing it with the aid of a watch you can find out how many times it goes around in a minute. When the revolutions are faster you will know the wind is stronger. If they are fewer you will know it is not so strong. The anemometer will respond to very small changes in the velocity of the wind—changes that would not otherwise be noticeable.

If you would rather use cones than funnels in your anemometer, it is quite simple to do. Tall tin fruit juice or canned chicken cans will provide a large enough tin sheet to make the cones. Prepare your sheet of tin in the same manner as described in the section on weather vane.

From paper cut a circle with its diameter equaling the height of the can, which will be just short of seven inches or about six and five-eighths inches. Then cut out a section equal to one-quarter of the circle.

Paste this cone pattern on your tin plate and cut it out with tin snips. Bring the edges together until they overlap about one-eighth of an inch at the circumference and solder the seam together. The result will be a cone almost five inches in diameter across the open end.

(For method of soldering seam, refer to seam soldering in the Tin-Can Craft section.)

THE RAIN GAUGE

After every big rainstorm people talk about how much it rained. Sometimes the rainfall makes the headlines. "Almost an inch of rain fell in yesterday's storm." Wouldn't it be fun to measure the rainfall yourself? You can do it with an exceptionally simple instrument.

You need only a quart-sized milk bottle and a funnel, but in buying the funnel be careful. The diameter of the funnel at its top must be the same as the inside of the milk bottle. Set this rain catcher out when it starts to rain. When the storm is over measure the amount of water in the milk bottle. Also add ten per cent to compensate for the rain that splashes outside the funnel when it strikes.

If you jot down the amount of rainfall after each storm in a notebook and at the end of the season total all your figures, your total of the season's rainfall will be surprisingly accurate. It will be fun to check your figures with that of the local weather bureau.

It is much easier to realize the amount of snowfall than rainfall and yet that too can be very deceptive, especially if the ground is already covered with snow. If you live in the land of winter ice and snow, perhaps you'd enjoy measuring snow also. Put an empty bucket or pail out when it starts to snow. When it has stopped measure the fall with a yardstick.

Because freshly fallen snow is apt to be light and fluffy with a large amount of air in and between the flakes it takes more snow than rain to provide an equal amount of moisture. About one foot of snow equals one inch of rain. In charting the amount of annual precipitation, it will be necessary to remember this.

FLORAL BAROMETER

Would you like to be able to tell when it is going to rain? It is very easy with a floral barometer. Make a bouquet of pink and blue crepe paper flowers and dip them in cobalt chloride. When it is going to rain the pink flowers will stay pink and the blue flowers will remain blue. But if the weather is going to be dry the pink flowers will change to purple and the blue flowers to green.

You can get the pink and blue paper flowers at the variety store or you can make them quite easily. Use a strip of crepe paper about three feet long and three inches wide. Fold this strip crosswise in the center and refold it again and again until you have folded the strip five times. You will now have thirty-two thicknesses of paper folded into a small bundle. Cut one end of this folded strip to make a curving petal edge. After cutting, unfold the strip and you will have sixteen petals. Curl the edge of each petal by scraping the edges with a silver knife or the edge of the scissors. Gather the first four petals closely together and then gradually gather the others around so as to form a flower.

Cut a strip of green crepe paper, three inches long and two inches wide, into six sharp points. Wrap this green piece around the outside of the flower to form a calyx. Fasten one end of a piece of stiff wire to the flower for a stem and then wrap the wire with green crepe paper. The flower is finished.

Make several flowers of the pink crepe paper and several of the blue. Buy a small quantity of cobalt chloride at a drugstore and dissolve it in water. Then dip the flowers in the solution and let them dry. It may be necessary to dip the flowers several times if the solution is not strong. Be sure to let the flowers dry thoroughly after each bath.

Put the flowers in a vase and your floral barometer is now ready for use. Of course, you'll have to keep this barometer outdoors to accurately forecast rain.

CHEMICAL WEATHER GLASS

A weather glass will forecast change in weather, storm conditions, or fair weather. A chemical weather glass is very simple to make. All you need is an ordinary glass test tube about five inches long and one-half inch in diameter, although that need not be the exact size; a wooden block on which to mount it; and a few simple chemicals purchasable for a small amount at the corner drugstore.

The wooden block should be about one-half inch thick and just slightly longer than the glass tube, say an inch or so. It should be about three inches wide.

The first step is to paint or varnish the wooden block so that it will stand the weather. Next cut two narrow tin strips from an old tin can to strap the glass tube onto the wooden block; one strip near the bottom of the tube and one near the top.

The chemicals needed must be purchased at the drugstore, so doubtless the druggist will weigh and mix the chemicals for you. The formula consists of:

2 ounces of water
2 ounces of alcohol
½ dram of ammonium chloride
½ dram of potassium nitrate
2 drams of camphor

These chemicals must be completely dissolved and it may be necessary to shake them well in a bottle before filling the test tube. The tube should be filled within about three-fourths inch from the top and closed with a cork to keep the dust out.

Before mounting the tube on the block it is well to mark on the block a scale. Measure where the glass tube is to be. Then about one and one-fourth inches from the bottom draw a line and mark it FAIR. About one and one-eighth inches from the bottom line draw another line and mark it CHANGE. Add one more line two and one-fourth inches above the bottom line and mark it STORMY. When this is well marked you can shellac over it so that it will not weather.

Or you can make this scale on a piece of white paper —paste it on the wooden block in proper position and shellac it so that it will be permanent.

Then fasten the glass tube onto the block in a proper place with the scale. Your weather glass is now completed.

On clear days the liquid in your weather glass will appear to be absolutely clear. When the crystals show near the bottom — the weather glass indicates fair weather, with humid air in summer and heavy frost in winter.

When the liquid is sort of milky or dim then look out for bad weather. When the crystals rise in the tube and approach the point marked CHANGE, maybe a storm is on the way.

The tube full of crystals means storm for sure. As the weather clears the crystals will sink in the tube and pass the point marked CHANGE. This means that probably clear weather is on tap.

Why does this weather glass work? The answer is quite simple. If you have ever tried to dissolve salt in water you will discover that salt will dissolve better in warm water than in cold; that warm water will absorb more salt than cold water.

So it is with the solution in the chemical water glass. The amount of moisture in the air and slight changes in temperature affect the amount of the chemicals which the liquid can hold in solution. So on fair dry days the liquid will be clear and on others full of crystals.

Your weather glass is now ready to be hung wherever you wish, but the best place is on the north side of the house or at least in a shady spot where it is out of the direct rays of the sun.

WEATHER CHART

Now that you have all your instruments made it will be fun to keep track of your weather findings. By setting your findings down on a chart you will soon find that you too can forecast the weather with amazing accuracy. The chart is simple to make. Use a large sheet of heavy paper or cardboard—draw a line across the top and label it in bold letters — **W E A T H E R C H A R T**. Then divide the sheet into seven columns: **Date Barometer Wind Sky Temperature Humidity Forecast.**

Under the column labeled **Sky** is the place for your own observations of the heavens. For this, of course, no instrument is needed, but a bit of information about the clouds is helpful. There are four kinds of clouds, each of which is a weather indicator in itself. They are called cirrus, cumulus, stratus, and nimbus.

Cirrus clouds—the name CIRRUS means a "ringlet of hair." The delicate, feathery clouds, high in the sky, often look like tufts or curls of white hair. They are probably made up of tiny droplets in the form of ice crystals. They are formed by the condensing and freezing of moisture in the air currents which precede a storm area. Therefore, cirrus clouds are the forerunners of a storm.

Cumulus Clouds—the word CUMULUS means "a heap." These clouds were so named because they look like great heaps of wool. They are formed on warm days when the heated air rushes upward in tremendous currents. These clouds are formed by the condensing of moisture in the upward air currents. When these cumulus clouds are few and small and light in color they are a sign of fair weather, but when they become large and dark they are a sign of approaching storm. When they are large and dark we call these clouds thunderheads because it is from these clouds we get our sudden thunderstorms.

Stratus Clouds — These clouds appear to lie in layers not too high in the sky. Stratus clouds sometimes blanket the entire sky and shut off the direct sunlight, but they usually have little effect on the weather. They may last all day, but more often occur in the morning or early evening.

Nimbus Clouds — They are the real storm clouds, heavy with moisture. They are shapeless and ragged-looking, the lower part made up of falling raindrops. Nimbus clouds appear just before or during a severe storm. The combination of the dark, low-lying nimbus clouds against a background of gray stratus clouds adds to the dreary effect of a stormy day.

A record of the type of clouds visible on a given day will help you foretell the weather. Of course, if there are no clouds in sight, the word "clear" will help with the day's weather picture.

The space headed **Forecast** should contain your own opinion of the weather for the next 24 hours. If

GAMES FOR ALL AGES AND HOW TO USE THEM

you mark your forecast at approximately the same time each day, and then check it against the actual weather the next day, you'll soon learn to improve your observation powers and as a result the accuracy of your forecasting. Before long the minute you step outside you'll notice the wind direction, the temperature, the clouds and the sky. All your crowd will consult you as to the weather forecast.

18.

Tin Can Fun

When you help Dad haul the old tin cans out to the dump, chances are it never occurs to you that thousands of people are very much interested in using tin cans for their hobbies.

Working with metal has long been recognized as interesting and profitable, but the expense and difficulty of getting the usual materials of the metal craftsman (gold, silver, brass, copper, and pewter) has discouraged many a would-be metal worker. In lieu of expensive metals many people have turned to the lowly tin can for hobby material.

Tin cans are everywhere. They are made of pure tin covering a steel core and are the perfect material for anyone who wants to have fun with metal at little cost.

Entire books have been written about the elaborate articles that can be made from tin cans. But here we are going to tell you boys and girls what fun you can have with old tin cans—making stoves, steam turbines, lanterns, telephones, camp-cooking equipment, tin can stilts, and party horns.

Only a few tools and some know-how are needed. You will need a pair of tin snips, a hammer with a rounded end (ball-peen), a rather dull jack-knife for scraping, a file to smooth the edges, and a can opener that flattens the edge as it cuts the top off. You will also need a soldering iron. You can use the soldering point that comes with the iron in your burnt wood set.

Wash the can in hot water to remove the labels. If the top hasn't been entirely cut off, finish the job with a crank can opener to insure a smooth edge. Cut off the bottom with the same crank opener.

Open the can by cutting with the tin shears along one edge of the seam from top to bottom. When cutting be sure to hold the blades of the shears at right angles to the surface being cut. Otherwise, the tin is apt to buckle and not cut easily. Now cut the top and bottom ridges off as well as the seam edge.

As soon as the edges are cut scrape them well with your dull jack-knife to remove any possible sharp snags that may cut your fingers as you work. A file or a fine emery is used for a final finish. It is wise to hold the tin in a vise while filing or smoothing.

The rounded piece of tin must now be flattened. One way is to rub the curved side back and forth across the edge of a table or the work bench. Pull it back and forth slowly, gradually increasing pressure until the curve is rubbed out.

Another way is to lay the metal flat on the table and tap the curve with a wooden mallet. You now have a piece of tin plate ready for use.

To do a good job of soldering, whether it be a seam or two pieces of tin, it is important to have the tin pieces thoroughly clean. And do not forget the corners. Scrape until the metal shines. As solder will not adhere to a soiled surface, this step is very important. Scrub with a fine emery all parts to be soldered until they are bright and shiny. Avoid finger marks on the polished surfaces. Any oil, grease or dirt will keep the solder from sticking.

You can purchase a small amount of solder wire with flux in it. Hold the wire along the crack to be soldered, apply heat with the soldering iron until the wire melts and solders the crack. If you do not get the wire with flux in it, it will be necessary to buy a small amount of flux. Then brush or rub it on with a paddle. The flux prevents oxidizing which would keep solder from sticking. After applying the flux, solder with wire in place as described above.

A TIN CAN COOKING KIT

Perhaps you have wished for a camp-cooking outfit—the kind that nestles together and is easily carried. Such a camp-cooking kit can be yours for the making. First locate the size of cans that will fit together. Start with a two-pound coffee can. The top edge is smooth and it has a cover to fit. Punch two holes—one in each side. The wire from a coat hanger makes an excellent bail. A No. 2½ can, such as contains fruit, will fit in next, and then the No. 2 can used usually for vegetables will fit nicely inside this. If in opening a can you have one of the rotary types of can opener, you will have a smooth rim. It is important to tap down any rough edges.

Most cooking kits have a stew kettle. A one-pound coffee can serves as an excellent stew kettle. Add the wire bail and your stew kettle is complete.

Drinking cups can be made from the ordinary vegetable can. With tin snips make a straight cut down the side of the can until it is within two inches of the bottom of the can. Make a parallel cut leaving a strip one and one-half inches wide to form the handle.

Then cut around the can two inches from the bottom. You will now have a cup with a vertical handle. Cut a slit one-fourth inch on each side of the base of the handle and double the edges of the handle back. Then roll the handle back to make a small loop with which to hold the cup. Now snip at intervals of one inch the top edge of the cup to the depth of one-fourth inch. Then turn the tin down very carefully to form a smooth edge for the lips.

A skillet is made the same way as the drinking cup, only you start with a larger tin can. Cut a handle strip three inches wide, leaving the depth of the skillet about two inches. Snip the handle on each side of its base to a depth of one-half inch. Using a wire—coat hanger wire is good—along each edge of the handle, roll the edges of the handle back. Bend the ends of the wire at right angles to the skillet so as to strengthen the straight handle. The edge of the skillet is treated the same way as the drinking cup edge. Make quarter-inch snips an inch apart and fold the edge down to form a finished edge. The skillet handle may not be strong enough to lift the pan of food, but it will serve to hold the skillet and pull it off the fire.

A TIN CAN STOVE

The next time your crowd goes on a bike hike, why not take along a tin can stove? These amazing little stoves heat quickly with a small amount of fuel. A meal can be cooked in a minimum amount of time with no aftermath of dishwashing because the stove serves as a skillet too.

The best size can for a tin can stove is a No. 10 can. These cans are about seven inches high and six and three-sixteenths inches in diameter. They are used by canneries for vegetables and by dairies for powdered milk and ice cream mix. As they hold about a gallon of vegetables, the best place to get one is at your neighborhood restaurant. They will be glad to get rid of them.

It is best if the top hasn't been completely removed from your can but left attached on one side. At the top of the can with tin snips cut a three-inch doorway. At the bottom of the can on the opposite side of the doorway cut a hole about one and one-half inches square for a chimney.

Press the top of the can back in normal position, turn the can upside down and your stove is ready to use. Lay your fire with tinder and pencil-sized twigs. In seconds the top of your stove will be hot. The first time the stove is used, give it a good rubbing with a cloth to rub off any enamel that may be loose.

Lay bacon around the outer edge of your stove and use the center for frying eggs or cooking pancakes. Your meal will be done in no time at all. Watch your fingers because the stove gets very hot and the bacon grease might catch fire, although this small amount of grease burning will do no damage.

TIN CAN OVENS

There are two types of tin can ovens that are interesting and easy to make. Use the top of your stove to bake your biscuits. Use half of a second No. 10 can for a cover. Be sure to smooth all edges of your cut metal so as to avoid nasty cuts. This type of oven will do nicely for a small serving of biscuits.

Sooner or later every camper will want to bake a supply of biscuits. For this a reflector oven best answers his need. A honey of a reflector oven can be made from a large tin can—a five-quart lard pail, a large cookie can, or an even larger five-gallon motor oil can. Any large can with a removable cover will do. The first step is to cut with a can opener about one-third the distance around the bottom edge of the can. Then from the top with tin snips cut along the seam of the can to the bottom. Put the cover back on the can, bend the cut side in to form a flat surface on which to bake the biscuits. Your reflector oven is complete.

This oven can be set close to a hot fire, or over a bed of glowing coals. We guarantee your biscuits will be well done.

A TIN CAN LANTERN

While you are camping maybe you'd like to have a candle lantern. All you need is a big lard or honey pail, and a candle. Wash the can thoroughly, polishing the inside to serve as a reflector Then loosen the bail on one side and bring it around to fasten to the bottom rim, so that your can will be in a horizontal position with the bail on one side. Cut a hole in the now bottom side of the can through which you can insert your candle.

This lantern will throw more light than the average candle and the blaze will be protected from blowing curtains or clothing. Also the candle will not blow out easily as it will be protected from the wind.

A TIN CAN TELEPHONE

Tin cans are ideal, too, for making a string telephone. For this you need two tin cans, and about fifty feet of wire or string. String is perhaps the easiest to handle. Almost any size can will do, but in our illustration we used discarded vegetable tin cans.

Punch a hole in the exact center of the bottom of each of the two cans. Pull a string through the holes, knotting it on the inside of the can so it won't slip out.

Get your pal to hold one can as an ear phone—stretch the string taut. You can whisper into the other can and your friend at the other end of the line will hear you distinctly.

A word of warning! Do not put your fingers on the bottom of the can, but hold it as near the front edge of the can as possible. Fingers on the bottom of the can will muffle the sound.

A TIN HORN

A tin horn! You've heard of them—why not make one? If you want a small horn, use a large size tin can.

Open the can along the seam and trim both edges as described in preparing tin plate. Then shape a cone from the tin, soldering the seam together. The simplest mouthpiece is to get one from an old bugle. Insert it in the small end and you'll have a real party horn.

If you'd prefer a long lumberman's horn, it'll be necessary to solder together the tin from three large tin cans to form a long sheet. Then make a cone of it, soldering the seam. If the completed cone is six feet long, it should have a six-inch spread at the big end— a three-foot horn should be three inches at the big end, etc. Insert the bugle mouthpiece in the small end. With a little practice your fun will be unlimited.

A HALLOWEEN SQUAWKER

A squawker with an especially eerie sound is easily made from an ordinary tomato can, or any other about that size. First fashion a handle to insert in one side of the can. Whittle a wooden piece with a small projection to fit into the can. Or you can use a dowel about one inch in diameter and cut it down at one end so that it can be inserted in the can.

Next on the closed end of the can punch a hole large enough to thread a yard of kite string or fish line. Knot it securely on the inside of the can. Outside the can knot the string about every three or four inches in a tight knot. Rub the whole line with violin resin.

Draw tight over the open end of the can a piece of tissue paper and fasten it with rubber bands. If you hold the squawker by its handle and quickly draw the thumb and forefinger rapidly over the cord a roaring and barking sound will result. Your friends will think all the wild animals in the zoo are loose. We have found these squawkers especially useful on Halloween.

TIN CAN STILTS

Tin can stilts are fun. There are two ways of making them. The first is merely to fasten a five-inch wide strip of old inner tube to the closed end of the tin can. Races with these short tin can stilts are hilarious.

But if you would like taller stilts, for each stilt use two tin cans of matching size. Securely fasten into the first can four or five wooden slats. The length of the slats will determine the height of the stilt. Next fasten the inner tube stirrup into the second can with the closed end up. Slip this can onto the top end of the slats and screw them securely with drive screws. Make your second stilt to match and you can go high walking down the street.

HAMBURGER ROASTER

Cut a tin can open and flatten it. Using the round head of a ball peen hammer make three impressions in the tin about the size of a hamburger. This is easily done by holding the tin over a log with a hollow in it.

Then take a wire coat hanger and bend the part below the hook into the shape of a rectangle. Lay it over the flattened tin. Roll the edges of the tin over the coat hanger and you are all set with a grill in which to fry hamburgers.

WATER DRUM

For this unique drum cut the top off a tin can. Fill the can about one third full of water. Stretch a chamois tightly over the open end and tie it securely around the can.

For a drum stick, pad the end of a stick with cotton, and cover it with a piece of cloth. Tie securely. Now you are all set to boom away on your water drum.

19.

Charades

Everyone at heart is an actor—and charades give us all an opportunity to show our talents in the center of the stage. Charades are usually done in pantomime, but occasionally call for a verbal bit. However they are done, they are fun for the actor and good sport for the crowd.

NOVEL CHARADES

This is best played by a group of adults or older young people who are familiar with many books of fiction. Beforehand the leader writes off on two sheets of paper a scene from a book such as Tom Sawyer or Peyton Place. At the party two players are given the manuscripts and read the lines, with as much action as they can muster on such short notice.

The rest of the group name the book from which the scene is taken. It is an exciting game if the scenes are chosen from all types of books. It can be made easier if the scenes are restricted to one type such as best sellers, or to classical books, or to juveniles.

Not more than ten scenes should be enacted. Otherwise, the game might get tiresome. At the close of the acting, the leader reads the correct answers and a prize is awarded the one with the most nearly correct list. For extra fun have the group vote for the one who did the best acting of the chosen part.

A DOG'S LIFE

Each player draws a slip of paper (which has been prepared ahead of time) from a hat. On each slip is described a situation to be acted out, in bow-wow language only, by the person drawing it. Here are some good situations:

Bing Crosby singing a sentimental ballad.

A bashful boy explaining to teacher why he was late to school.

A boy teasing to play out after dark with the crowd.

A mother scolding her small son for breaking a window.

A father refusing to increase his son's allowance.

The trick is to guess what situation is being portrayed by the person barking through his assignment. The one doing the best job of explaining his situation in dog language is awarded a bag of dog biscuits. The player making the sharpest guest is also awarded dog biscuits.

FAMILY SECRETS

Let one member of the family group imitate some other member of his particular family in some activity and the crowd guess what it is. For instance, young John may imitate his sister primping for a date. Dad may impersonate mother entertaining the minister at tea. Mother may retaliate by showing Dad trying to borrow a "Five" from Uncle George.

PAPER BAG CHARADE

Divide your crowd into groups of four or five. Give each group a paper bag into which you have put ten unrelated items, such as a potato, a pencil, an eraser, a paper clip, a fork, a button, a notebook, a rubber band, some string, and a peanut.

Each group is then asked to make up a skit using all the items in its bag. Prizes can be given the group doing the best job.

WORD CHARADE

Party is divided into several groups. Each group chooses a word and acts it out in syllables—then as a whole word. The watchers try to guess word each group has chosen.

Some suggested words to use:

Message (Mess, Age)
Wonderful (One, Dear, Full)
Truant (True, Ant)
Tuberculosis (Tube, Irk, You, Low, Sis)
Sausage (Saw, Sage)
Interne (Inn, Turn)
Pumpkin (Pump, Kin)
Handkerchief (Hand, Cur, Chief)
Pillow (Pill, Low)
Utensil (You, Ten, Sill)

SLOGAN CHARADE

This form of charade is one frequently played on television. Party is divided into two teams. A list of slogans or sayings, or familiar quotations are written on slips of paper and put in a hat. Member No. One of the first team draws a slip and acts out the slogan. The team first to guess the slogan scores. Then Member No. One of the second team takes a turn, etc.

For these longer sentences, signals have been worked out to help the guessers. The pantomimist indicates the number of words in the slogan by holding up the same number of fingers. Any key word of the slogan can be acted out first, but the actor indicates with fingers which word is being acted, and then which syllable.

Small words, such as "and," "of," "a," "the," "but" and "for" are shown by holding the thumb and index finger about an inch apart. If someone gets close to the right answer, the actor lets him know by pointing to him and then waving to himself as an indication for more guesses along that line. No props are used. No words are spoken—everything is done in pantomime.

DOG'S DAY

Give each guest a slip of paper on which is typed a stunt similar to these:

> Imitate a dog meeting a cat
> Imitate a dog gnawing on a bone
> Imitate a dog howling at the moon
> Imitate a dog in a dog fight
> Imitate a dog chasing its tail
> Imitate a dog barking at a squirrel up a tree
> Imitate a dog greeting its master.

As each stunt is performed the rest try to guess what the actor is doing.

Index